Crosscurrents / MODERN CRITIQUES

Harry T. Moore, *General Editor*

Eric Thompson

T. S. Eliot

THE METAPHYSICAL PERSPECTIVE

WITH A PREFACE BY

Harry T. Moore

SOUTHERN ILLINOIS UNIVERSITY PRESS
Carbondale and Edwardsville

FEFFER & SIMONS, INC.
London and Amsterdam

PREFACE

AMONG ALL the books on T. S. Eliot, Eric Thompson's is just now the latest. Its raison d'être is that it presents fresh data, perspectives and evaluations.

The late T. S. Eliot is a world figure of startling dimension. Startling, that is, to those of us who can remember the time when he was, despite his great gifts, comparatively unknown.

In the 1920s, The Waste Land was of course known in university and other intellectual circles, and it won the Dial Award, whose $2,000 must have been most welcome to the young poet and publishers' assistant. By 1932 he was fairly well known in the American colleges; that was the year in which, as Norton Lecturer at Harvard, he made his first visit to his native country in eighteen years. Sometime in 1932–33 he went to Los Angeles and spoke at U. C. L. A. His lecture was rather well attended, partly because he gave it in the morning, at student-assembly time; the large auditorium was crowded. Eliot read parts of The Waste Land, with precisely the right shade of weariness in his voice, and he spoke of the poetic experience. It was an interesting occasion; one of my teachers, the poet and translator, C. F. McIntyre, later announced in class that he was annoyed because a native of St. Louis, in speaking of the Alps, had said "ma-oontins." Nevertheless, C. F. M. must have been impressed, for in his Poems (Macmillan, 1936), he used two fragments of Eliot's own poems as epigraphs.

A few nights after the U. C. L. A. lecture, Eliot spoke at the University of Southern California. The subject— Swinburne, Lear, and Carroll as nonsense-verse practition- ers—was perhaps unsympathetic, and it was in any event an off-campus day for most members of a city univer- sity, so that there wasn't much of a crowd for Mr. Eliot's Sunday evening service, held safely enough in a tiny hall. I don't know what kind of audiences he drew at Harvard that year, but they were probably large—though certainly not comparable with those he attracted there when he came back after another eighteen years. (By 1958 he was really packing them in; twenty thousand reported at Uni- versity of Minnesota and, at Southern Methodist Univer- sity in Dallas, about seven thousand people attended.)

As a student at Harvard, Eliot had been a member of the famous class of 1910, which included Heywood Broun, Stuart Chase, Walter Lippmann, and John Reed. Eliot contributed various poems to the Harvard Advocate, most of which were reprinted in a special Eliot issue in 1938; some of these and a few others, including a prose piece, appear in Donald Hall's The Harvard Advocate Anthology (Twayne, 1950). Although Eliot became secretary of the Advocate, he devoted himself to his studies with enough zeal to complete his undergraduate work in three years, taking his master's degree in the fourth.

Note that the subtitle of the present book is The Meta- physical Perspective: despite his early interest in French poets such as Laforgue, Eliot was absorbed in the study of metaphysics. After a year at the Sorbonne he returned to Harvard to study for his doctoral degree. His thesis, mailed from England in 1916, was on Experience and the Ob- jects of Knowledge in the Philosophy of F. H. Bradley. It was accepted at once by the Division of Philosophy, as Mr. Thompson notes in the following pages; Josiah Royce praised it highly. So did Conrad Aiken, many years later, in his autobiographical Ushant (1952), in which T. S. Eliot is called "the Tsetse": Aiken characterizes the dis- sertation as "the Tsetse's brilliantly analytic and destruc- tive thesis in epistemology."

Eliot has said that it was accepted because it was unreadable. He never returned to Harvard to receive the Ph. D. that would have been his if he had only made the routine appearance required by ritual. The thesis rested for many years in that residence hall named for a relative of his, Eliot House; the document was eventually removed to the Houghton Library, Harvard. In 1964 the dissertation was published in the United States by Farrar, Straus, but how many of its purchasers have found it "unreadable"— or the opposite—is not known.

In the present book, Eric Thompson valuably investigates that little-known, "unreadable" dissertation which gives so many indications of Eliot's ideational-poetic development. As Mr. Thompson points out, the Bradley scholar R. W. Church wrote of the thesis appreciatively in the Eliot number of the Advocate in 1938, but Kristian Smidt and Hugh Kenner, who have investigated Eliot's relationship to Bradley, apparently didn't see the text of this dissertation. Mr. Thompson's exploration of it is one of the notable contributions of his book. He provides background information about Bradley himself, he discusses Eliot's thesis on Bradley, and then he traces the influence of Bradley on Eliot's poetry.

I'll let Mr. Thompson have his own say about these matters; I am interested, as the writer of the preface to what is just now the latest book on Eliot, in that growth of the poet's reputation I mentioned earlier. Readers of our time have seen various minority writers become, in common esteem, major authors, but in most cases this change has occurred after the writers' deaths. Joyce and Lawrence, for example, who are now so dominant in American classrooms—no Nobel Prizes for them, nor for Proust, as far as that goes. But the Nobel thing has become a joke: in 1962, for example, it was awarded to John Steinbeck, at a time when such American writers as Robert Frost, Lewis Mumford, and Thornton Wilder, to take three of them alphabetically, were so notably eligible. It seems fantastic that the Nobel Prize was once awarded to Pearl S. Buck: how Mary Roberts Rinehart, Margaret Mitchell, or Zane Grey

missed it is something to wonder over. Joyce, who had little enough money most of his life, even from the contra-
band Ulysses, had to submit himself for years to what
Thornton Wilder has called "the appalling treadmill of the
Berlitz schools"; and later Joyce was supported by Edith
Rockefeller McCormick and Harriet Shaw Weaver. Lawrence, in his youth put out of schoolmastering by ill
health, for many years lived frugally on his earnings as a
writer until, at the end of his life, he cleverly supervised
the publication of the privately printed Florentine edition
of Lady Chatterley's Lover; that hardly made him rich,
and it made him more infamous than famous. No, there
was no best selling and there were no prizes for a number
of the writers of only a few years ago whom we now recognize as having written importantly about our own age.

No one would seriously say that T. S. Eliot didn't deserve the Nobel award. He lived on, as I pointed out
earlier, into world fame. This must astonish those who
knew him in his earlier days, when he was a minority figure. If he had returned to America for his Ph. D., he
might have become a college professor over here; to speculate as to what his future might have been would be as
idle as indulging in such suppositions as those of the kind
James Thurber kidded forever in "If Grant Had Been
Drunk at Appomatox." So let's look at the actuality of
Eliot's experience.

He had at first disliked England; as he told Conrad
Aiken, "a people which is satisfied with such disgusting
food is not civilized." But after the coming of war had
driven him out of Germany (he had been studying at Marburg), he went to Merton College, Oxford, to read metaphysics; and he has been an Englishman ever since. For a
while he was an usher in Highgate Junior School, where
he was known as "the American Master"; one of the students there who remembers him from 1914–15 is John
Betjeman, who in his autobiographical poem, Summoned
by Bells, speaks of "That dear, good man with Prufrock in
his head / And Sweeney waiting to be agonized. . . ."
Actually, Prufrock was not only in Eliot's head at that

time; it was already on paper, one of the brilliant 1910–11 poems Mr. Thompson analyzes early in the present volume. "The Love Song of J. Alfred Prufrock" appeared first in Harriet Monroe's Poetry in 1915.

After ushering at Highgate, Eliot became a clerk in Lloyds Bank, Ltd., but the death that undid so many did not undo him. His first volume, Prufrock and Other Observations, was brought out in 1917 by the Egoist Press. Clive Bell has recalled taking an armful of copies to Lady Ottoline Morrell's country-house salon at Garsington Manor, Oxford, where he distributed them to his hostess and her husband, Philip Morrell, to Mary Hutchinson, Aldous Huxley, Katherine Mansfield, Middleton Murry, and (probably) Mark Gertler; Katherine Mansfield read "Prufrock" aloud. They liked it, and Eliot became a part of the Garsington crowd (though a prominent member of its city cousin, the Bloomsbury group, assures me that Eliot never quite belonged to the latter, whose existence as a group is in any event denied by Clive Bell himself). Those people in the deckchairs listening to Katherine Mansfield as she read "Prufrock" on the lawn at Garsington—the Breadalby of Lawrence's Women in Love—could hardly have foreseen that Eliot's fame would one day eclipse that of them all.

Some interesting notes on the early stages of Eliot's reputation occur in Life For Life's Sake (Viking Press, 1941), that wryly amusing and undeservedly neglected autobiography of Richard Aldington's which has never even been printed in his native England—because, Aldington told me, of a publisher's belief that Aldington's statements about Gilbert Cannan are libelous (which they are not; they defend Cannan, and give an opposite point of view from those expressed in Middleton Murry's autobiography, which was printed in England as well as America). Aldington in Life For Life's Sake speaks of Eliot in 1919 as "almost unknown and having rather a rough time." Publication of his poems had brought on violent antagonism; one ancient expert on the eighteenth century even said they were written by a "drunken helot." Under British law, this was actionable because it was a derogation of character; but Eliot, as Aldington notes, "very wisely did nothing at all."

In the early 1920s, Aldington was reviewing French literature for the Times Literary Supplement. When he learned that its editor, Bruce Richmond, was looking for a leader writer, he suggested Eliot. But Eliot's detractors had Richmond's ear; and Eliot on his part wouldn't go to the editor hat in hand. Aldington finally arranged for the two men to meet for lunch at a tavern just after Eliot's return from Switzerland. While there, Eliot had grown an Uncle Sam beard, and when he turned up for the lunch "he looked perfectly awful, like one of those comic-strip caricatures of Southern hicks." As Richmond shook his head and blinked, Aldington felt that his own good intentions had crashed. But, "over a steak and a pewter pot of bitter, Eliot began talking. In five minutes he had completely captivated Richmond, as he can captivate any intelligent person." Later, Richmond made a discreet Oxonian jest about the beard, and "when we next met Tom it had vanished." And Eliot became a TLS leader writer.

He has of course continued to have detractors, even in the days of his great fame. Rossell Hope Robbins' The T. S. Eliot Myth (Schuman, 1951) concentrates much of the opposition and attacks the Eliot cult. The Sweeniad (Sagamore Press, 1957), by "Myra Buttle," is a satire not quite funny enough to do more than emphasize the fact that T. S. Eliot is an institution that can be satirized. One of his books which aroused great antagonism—largely because of its tone—was Notes Toward the Definition of Culture, which came out in 1948, the year in which he was awarded the Nobel Prize.

The Nobel Prize and the play, The Cocktail Party, first produced in 1949, brought Eliot his really great fame. After its first performances at the Edinburgh Festival, The Cocktail Party became a raging success on Broadway and on Shaftesbury Avenue—which takes us far away indeed from the Prufrock of the Garsington lawns.

In 1950, Eliot came to America to deliver the first Theodore Spencer Memorial Lecture, "Poetry and Drama." It was to be given at four p. m. in Sanders Theatre. Arriving a little before two, I thought I would be in good time to get a seat. But Sanders had been packed since morning; I soon became part of an enormous crowd around Memorial Hall. Finally we were all admitted to a huge room down the hall from Sanders, and a loudspeaker was set up so that we could hear the poet even if we couldn't see him. During his smooth and witty lecture, I kept thinking of Garsington, and Katherine Mansfield reading "The Love Song of J. Alfred Prufrock" to Lady Ottoline's coterie. And I also kept thinking of what had just been said outside Memorial Hall by one of the astonished Cambridge policemen who was trying to keep the mob under control: "Who's this guy, Eliot?"

Certain matters connected with this poet's publication in America may seem as baffling to the reader of Eliot as his identity was to the policemen outside Sanders Theatre. For example, in The Mentor Book of Major American Poets (New American Library, 1961), Edwin Honig and the late Oscar Williams, included a "Special Note From the Editors." This expressed their regret that T. S. Eliot wasn't represented in the volume. His American publishers—Harcourt, Brace and World—had announced that his work could not appear in paperback anthologies which sold for "less than $2.50." Subsequently these publishers notified Messrs. Williams and Honig, "It is our policy not to allow Mr. Eliot's poetry to appear in paperback books selling for less than $1.75." Interesting figure, at any rate; how was it determined?

Eleven days after their $1.75 ultimatum, Harcourt, Brace and World told the Mentor editors, "We must refuse permission for Mr. Eliot's work to appear in paperback books intended for the mass market." Notes for the definition of culture, indeed! Though it must be made clear that Oscar Williams later exonerated Eliot, stating that it was not the poet but his American publishers who had made the determinations about paperback appearances.

Now what is all this nonsense about "the mass market"?

Superficially and immediately, it doesn't seem like a publisher's greed, since theoretically the mass market would have more money to spend. But wait a minute: the demand for Eliot's writings is great, so there will be a mass market for them even in more expensive editions.

Regrettably, publishing has in our time become a major industry. Many of us in the area of twentieth-century literature have refused to edit textbooks in that field because the permission fees are too high to make such ventures worth one's time. At one level, it's good to see that authors are getting repaid for reprints of their work; but in many cases the author is dead, and his papers are being clutched by an ancient Juliana Bordereau. We can all remember Yvor Winters' book on the bachelor Edwin Arlington Robinson (New Directions, 1946), which had to be printed without quotations from the poetry of Robinson. As for the Mentor anthology which couldn't include Eliot's work—Robinson Jeffers was similarly refused appearance by Random House, though Jeffers is in a state of comparative obscurity, and one might suppose that his publishers would want to give it a bit of an airing. Further, Messrs. Williams and Honig were permitted to use only a part of the material they had selected from Robert Frost and W. H. Auden. What goes?

My objections are those of a university teacher who wants to present to his students the finest writings of the twentieth century. But the publishers are making this less and less possible. Books have become so expensive that students can afford to buy only a few each semester; consequently, studies in an important area must be curtailed. Why are Eliot and some other modern authors being priced out of the student's market? Many of us would like this answered, since inflation in the book industry has so greatly increased the student's classroom expenses.

Among the ironies in the foregoing, note that the Williams-Honig editorial comment explains the absence of Eliot and the mere partial presence of Auden. Now one might ask the editors what goes with them—for their volume is called The Mentor Book of Major American Poets, and if Auden is an American, what is Eliot? Auden has been an American citizen since 1946; Eliot has been an English citizen since 1927. You can't have it both ways, editors, though the voracious American-literature teachers (the present writer is one of them) all too often try to do so. The point is that, just as Joseph Conrad doesn't belong to Polish literature, so—if the split between these disciplines continues—T. S. Eliot, like Henry James, belongs to English literature.

Well, whatever the geography of Eliot, and whatever the extent of his fame, Eric Thompson has written a fine and perceptive book on his work. Indeed, it is one of the most valuable studies of Eliot yet made, particularly in its thorough exploration of Burnt Norton. But it is all first rate, and the Bradley material is of special importance. This book is crucial to the full understanding of what T. S. Eliot has written.

HARRY T. MOORE

December 24, 1962

Note

Eric Thompson's excellent book on T. S. Eliot, first issued eight years ago, is deservedly going into still another edition, for it continues to be a valuable guide to Eliot's writings. In the foregoing Preface I noted that Richard Aldington's autobiography had not been published in England; it has recently been brought out over there.

H. T. M.

Southern Illinois University
December 1969

ACKNOWLEDGMENTS

THE PASSAGES QUOTED from T. S. Eliot's, "The Love Song of J. Alfred Prufrock," "Portrait of a Lady," "La Figlia che Piange," "Whispers of Immortality," *The Waste Land, Ash-Wednesday,* "Marina," "Sweeney Agonistes," *Burnt Norton, East Coker, Dry Salvages, Little Gidding, The Family Reunion,* and *The Cocktail Party* are taken from *The Complete Poetry and Plays,* 1952, published by Harcourt, Brace and Company, Inc. Permission to quote has been granted by T. S. Eliot and the publishers. Quotations from the following essays, "Ben Jonson," "The Function of Criticism," "Modern Education and the Classics," "The 'Pensées' of Pascal," "Shakespeare," "Thoughts after Lambeth," and "William Blake," are taken from T. S. Eliot's *Selected Essays,* New Edition, 1950, also published by Harcourt, Brace and Company. Publication of these quotations is by permission of the author and publisher.

I acknowledge with thanks the courtesy of T. S. Eliot and the Master of Eliot House, Professor J. H. Finley, who in 1949 gave me permission to study the manuscript of *Experience and the Objects of Knowledge in the Philosophy of F. H. Bradley* when it was in the Eliot House at Harvard. I wish to thank the officials of Houghton Library for making the document available for study when it came into their keeping. Inasmuch as Mr. Eliot does not permit quotation of the treatise, my description of it must be regarded as a free translation, what Josiah Royce would have called an "interpretation." For formulations of the metaphysical issues, neither Mr. Eliot nor Bradley should be held responsible.

Announcement of the forthcoming publication of T. S. Eliot's *Knowledge and Experience in the Philosophy of F. H. Bradley* was received as this book was being printed. If, as seems likely, this is to be the publication of Eliot's manuscript on Bradley, we may feel grateful that at last one of the pieces most necessary to seeing Eliot's work as a whole is to be made public.

Passages in Chapter 2 by Conrad Aiken and Wyndham Lewis are from *T. S. Eliot, a Symposium,* and are used by permission of Henry Regnery Company. The quotations are taken from the edition published by P L Editions Poetry, London. The material from Professor Costello's recollections of Josiah Royce's seminar in comparative methodology is published by permission of the Directors of the *Journal of Philosophy.* Material from Alan Wood's *Bertrand Russell* is printed by permission of Simon and Schuster, Inc.

An epigraph taken from George Santayana's *Three Philosophical Poets* and another from Stephen C. Pepper's *The Basis of Criticism in the Arts* are reprinted by permission of Harvard University Press.

For encouragement at the School of Letters, State University of Iowa, I thank Seymour M. Pitcher and Austin Warren, and from the Department of Philosophy, Gustav Bergmann whose charity in driving me through Bradley I still remember. To David Owen, of Syracuse University, who took the trouble to read the manuscript and comment, I am much indebted.

I am indebted also to the Research Committee of Ohio University and the President's Office for preparing the manuscript, and to the Ohio University Library for continuous assistance over a period of years.

CONTENTS

INTRODUCTION

IN APRIL 1916, T. S. Eliot mailed across the Atlantic from England a doctoral dissertation titled "Experience and the Objects of Knowledge in the Philosophy of F. H. Bradley" that was promptly read by the Division of Philosophy at Harvard and accepted, as Professor James H. Wood wrote to Eliot in June, without hesitation. Josiah Royce spoke of it as the work of an expert.[1] Several years ago when I read this document (it was then in the Eliot House; now it is in the Houghton Library), it seemed interesting to anyone interested in Eliot as a literary theorist and Eliot as a highly self-conscious philosophical poet. Just what the relation was between the writer of this technical treatise on epistemology and the poet who had seen "Prufrock" printed in *Poetry* a year before was not clear. Not clear as well was how anyone would ever tell another person what the substance of the treatise is. Only two persons seemed to have treated of it with appreciation: Conrad Aiken, who must have studied it while it was being written, for he spoke in his autobiography of its powerful influence on him;[2] R. W. Church, an F. H. Bradley scholar, who wrote a brief resumé of the work for *The Harvard Advocate* in 1938.[3]

Though most Eliot scholars seemed to know of the manuscript, few appeared to have studied it. Hugh Kenner and Kristian Smidt, whose investigations brought them closest to the relation of Bradley and Eliot, appeared not to have read the dissertation.[4] Finding the work significant, I thought I would like to give an account of it, and then hazard a suggestion as to the relation of the work to Eliot's criticism and his poetry. The following study is the result.

As might be expected, several points are at stake, though it may be that the points themselves are not what is important. The first is that Eliot's "real" beginning as a poet is a metaphysical perspective. This point seems to involve something of a paradox since, so far as anyone can see, Eliot wrote five poems that are the work of a master in 1910–11, and did not really settle down to the study of philosophy until 1911–15. But the beginning that I speak of as "real" is like that that Eliot speaks of in *Little Gidding:*

> *What we call the beginning is often the end*
> *And to make an end is to make a beginning.*
> *The end is where we start from.*

In Eliot's earliest poem in *The Complete Poems and Plays*, he has the metaphysical point of view spoken of. How he came to get it, how it happens to be at work in "Conversation Galante" and not in his apprentice poems, I do not know. But there it is as it is in "Prufrock," "Portrait of a Lady," "Preludes," and "La Figlia." Such a beginning, of course, is not what Aristotle would call a material, but a final cause. And so Eliot's philosophical studies between 1911 and 1915 are, not the finding of a point of view, but the testing and justifying of one. In the dissertation, which he must have started in 1911, although he did not finish it evidently until 1916, Eliot may have been doing what F. H. Bradley suggests every metaphysician does, finding bad reasons for believing what the poet knew on instinct.[5]

The second point is a corollary of the first: it is that though Eliot's philosophical studies may have been motivated by the idea that a scholarly young man might become a teacher of philosophy, his studies may, at a deeper level, have been part of the poet's hope to continue to be a poet after the age of twenty-five. This is not to deny that Eliot had a taste for metaphysical speculation. He has acknowledged that while studying philosophy his studies *were* his life.[6] Nevertheless, everything points, it would seem, to the fact that Eliot's bent after 1910 was toward a career as a man of letters, not as a philosopher. And here my second thesis intrudes, which is that Eliot became a philosopher in order to keep the poet in himself alive.

This leads to a third and last generalization. Eliot is commonly said to be a difficult poet and the reason often given is that he is a refined sensibility in a complex age.[7] I do not see why a refined sensibility in a complex age might not turn out poetry that is simple, sensuous, and passionate. Eliot is difficult, not because he knows so much or the age is so complex, but because he is a special sort of poet, a philosophical poet in an age of unbelief. Dante is a philosophical poet and Dante can be difficult enough; but there is not the discrepancy in Dante between what his materials say and what his form says that I seem to find in Eliot. Eliot is like one who takes his material from the blackened street, and uses a heap of broken bones to reconstruct a once beautiful body. This makes him difficult.

So much for the points that seem to emerge from this study: Eliot's beginning as a poet is a philosophical standpoint; Eliot's philosophical education was ultimately motivated by the need to be a poet; and Eliot's unique achievement is to be a philosophical poet in an age of unbelief. In order to work up these three points I have tried to investigate, first, Eliot's doctoral dissertation, then, his early criticism, and, then, the first of his *Four Quartets*, *Burnt Norton*. To justify this restriction of focus to three points in Eliot's career, I have wanted to believe that they are like three "middles" in his life, and that the person who would study all of Eliot, must start with these three middles. Eliot's treatise on Bradley, for example, is a middle between his early outburst of major poetry, 1910–11, and the outburst of early criticism, 1917–20. This criticism, which attracted attention to the poet, is the middle between the philosophical studies and *The Waste Land*, the work that made Eliot famous. That poem, without much doubt, is the realization of an ambition that Eliot must have been nursing for a long time; it may be the greatest philosophical poem in English. But I pass it by because it does not seem to be a completely public poem, as the *Four Quartets* are. I take *Burnt Norton* as the third middle because it occurs very interestingly in Eliot at the end of his first stage of development and the beginning of his latest. In some ways it is the most interesting and difficult of Eliot's mid-points.

These three middles constitute the core of the investigation. In the first we see Eliot committing himself consciously to a metaphysical perspective. In the second we see him working out an aesthetic for himself. In the third we see him making something very like Kierkegaard's movement of infinite resignation—he gives up the "poet" in himself and then receives him back.[8]

What is the value of approaching Eliot from the standpoint of his metaphysical standpoint? Several answers are possible. First, by this approach we can contribute to a theory of literature. Eliot is an admirable poet for the theorist to study just because he is so conscious. Second, we can throw light from a new angle on how to read a difficult poet. Many books have been written on Eliot, so many in fact that the feeling in some quarters is that interpretation has done its work.[9] It is possible to believe, however, that interpretations of Eliot are less satisfactory, on the whole, than the interpretations of almost any other contemporary poet. He is a *philosophical* poet; but he is a philosophical *poet*. He requires a double vision. In *The Waste Land*, for example, one must be inside the mind of the suffering Fisher King, and outside with the onlooking Teresias, in whom the truth is inborn, and who knows what has happened and what is going to happen. Few commentators have found a way to show what they see from two positions at once. This is what is attempted in the final essay on *Burnt Norton*.

ERIC THOMPSON

Ohio University

T. S. Eliot

THE METAPHYSICAL PERSPECTIVE

The reasonings and investigations of philosophy are arduous, and if poetry is to be linked with them, it can be artificially only, and with a bad grace. But the vision of philosophy is sublime. The order it reveals in the world is something beautiful, tragic, sympathetic to the mind, and just what every poet, on a small or on a large scale, is always trying to catch.— George Santayana, *Three Philosophical Poets*.

1 BACKGROUND TO THE STANDPOINT

Eliot's beginning as a poet, then, is a metaphysical standpoint. This is my first thesis at any rate. Such a beginning is not a cause as Monday night's low temperature is the cause of Tuesday's frozen water pipes; but perhaps we may grant that it is a beginning, the beginning of sight, and that that sight is what makes all of Eliot's work one work.

I had thought, originally, that to find Eliot's metaphysical perspective, we must proceed directly to his doctoral dissertation. But the logically straight line to the mark is not the learner's natural one. His interest in Eliot being largely literary, he knows the early poetry, "Prufrock" and so forth, but not the dissertation, and before being thrust into the mazes of Mr. Eliot's abstract metaphysics, he wants to be assured that there is some point in entering the labyrinth. Show us, he says, before we attempt to struggle through these abstractions, that there is a metaphysical standpoint in Eliot's earliest public verse, and that to know about it does a person some good. To meet that request is the purpose of this chapter.

First, however, before attempting to show that there is an ultimate standpoint in the earliest poems, let me suggest some of the difficulties of the term "standpoint." In Chapter 2, no term is more important, and I try to define it. But that definition occurs in a discussion of Eliot's epistemological treatise. How does the term apply to the poet?

It designates the part of the man that exists only as an

eye-seeing.[1] In the early criticism, on several occasions, Eliot uses the term "point of view." Conrad, he says, has a point of view; sometimes, wrongly Eliot says, called a philosophy, it makes all of Conrad's work a world.[2] Elsewhere when Eliot discriminates between an artist's point of view and a philosophy, he does so in such a way as to disparage the latter.[3] The element that Eliot here calls the artist's "point of view" is what F. H. Bradley evidently saw the metaphysician starting *with*; it is the instinct that the metaphysician spends his life finding bad reasons for believing in.

What is the relation between this mysterious entity in the poet as poet and the poet as man? Perhaps George H. Mead's distinction between a man's "I" and his "me" helps us here: [4] The "I" is that which forever focuses and evaluates events, but is itself never focused. The "me" on the other hand is a public image, a social role assigned us by other persons that we more or less accept. Eliot time and time again draws the important distinction between the artist's self who exists only as an eye-seeing, and the self which is the man.[5] Only when the experiences of the man are regarded as material for vision is the man an artist.

Approaching Eliot, we need to discriminate between the Eliot "I" and the Eliot "me." From 1910–16 the "I" is disclosed in the design of certain poems and in the cogitations that constitute the dissertation; that is the metaphysical Eliot. The "me" is visible now as an image in the letters and recollections of friends, a physical presence somewhat given to donning costumes and playing roles that bear only an indirect relation to the "I." To resurrect him briefly at this point is only for purposes of transcending him. Here are several random exposures of that Eliot.

Conrad Aiken, 1911–12.

> He had returned to Cambridge and Harvard to work for his doctorate in philosophy, returning already perceptibly Europeanized: he made a point, for a while, a conspicuously un-American point, of carrying a cane—was it a

malacca?—a little self-conscious about it, and complaining that its 'nice conduct' was no such easy matter. He had taken a room in Ash Street, installing in it a small stove— 'something to point the chairs at'—and a Gauguin *Crucifixion*, brought from Paris. The suggestion that the latter was a kind of sophisticated primitivism brought the reply, with a waspishness that was characteristic, that there 'was nothing primitive about it.' (A waspishness, let us say parenthetically, that has now and then got him into trouble: 'Shelley was a fool,' for example, or, of Chekhov, 'I prefer my Ibsen straight.') The boxing lessons, meanwhile, took place at a toughish gymnasium in Boston's South End, where, under the tutelage of an ex-pugilist with some such monicker as Steve O'Donnell, he learned not only the rudiments of boxing, but also, as he put it, 'how to swarm with passion up a rope'—his delight in this attainment was manifest. Was Steve O'Donnell the prototype of Sweeney, as some have suggested? Anyway, it was our habit to dine together after these gymnastic afternoons, usually at the Greek restaurant in Stuart Street, a small, dirty, and wonderfully inexpensive establishment which was in fact half restaurant and half pool-room; and it was here on one unfortunate occasion, when he had accidentally hit Steve too hard, that he turned up with a magnificent black eye, a shiner that did Steve great credit: it was really iridescent.[6]

H. T. Costello, 1913.

We had another student in the group in 1913–14, whom none of us thought of as a genius. I spelt his name "Eliott" instead of "Eliot" in my early notes, and knew him later as Tom Eliot from St. Louis. . . . His first paper was on the interpretation of primitive religions. He had been reading Durkheim, and Harrison, and Frazer, and wanted to know what is "interpretation" as opposed to "description"? His year's work circled around this question of the truth of interpretations. He had been reading Francis Herbert Bradley, and said no simple statement was absolutely true. Brogan, of course, [Albert P. Brogan] had to intervene to inquire if Eliot thought that last statement true? The argument waxed hot, and finally Eliot told Brogan, "You can't understand me. To understand my point of view, you have to believe it first." Royce intervened to say that a simple statement might be definitely true or false, except for the fact that we can never make a simple statement." [7]

Bertrand Russell, 1914 (from Alan Wood).

As well as his Lowell Lectures, Russell gave a course on Symbolic Logic, and invited his students to tea for informal discussions. In a letter written from Harvard at the time, he remarked that his students there were not very interesting or able, but that there were two exceptions. One was a Greek, Raphael Demos, later Professor of Philosophy at Harvard. T. S. Eliot was the second.[8]

Wyndham Lewis, January 1915.

As I entered the room I discovered an agreeable stranger parked up one of the sides of the triangle. He softly growled at me, as we shook hands. American. A graceful neck, I noted, with what elsewhere I have described as 'a Gioconda smile.' Though not feminine—besides being physically large his personality visibly moved within the male pale—there *were* dimples in the warm dark skin; undoubtedly he used his eyes a little like a Leonardo. He was a very attractive fellow then. . . . I liked him, though I may say not at all connecting him with texts Ezra had shown me about some fictional character dreadfully troubled with old age, in which the lines . . . 'I am growing old . . .' . . . I was unable to make head or tail of.

Ezra now lay flung back in typical posture of aggressive ease. . . . However, he kept steadily beneath his quizzical but self-satisfied observation his latest prize, or discovery— the author of *Prufrock*. The new collector's-piece went on smiling and growling out melodiously his apt and bright answers to promptings from the exhausted figure of his proud captor.[9]

Conrad Aiken again, 1914.

The beginning of the war, too, which was to wash Eliot up in London, back from Marburg, where he had just begun his studies, and myself in Boston. Where to live? The letters are full of the question. England was clearly impossible. 'A people which is satisfied with such disgusting food is *not* civilized.' London is at first detested. But Oxford and Merton with its 'Alexandrian verse, nuts, and wine,' the professors with pregnant wives and sprawling children, and hideous pictures on their walls, makes him long even for London, perhaps to work in the British Museum.[10]

Bertrand Russell again, 1915 (from Alan Wood).

> After Russell had returned to England, T. S. Eliot himself came to Europe; and one day they met by chance in a street near the British Museum, Russell having gone out to buy some milk for his tea. They went back together to Russell's flat in Bury Street. When Eliot married, Russell suggested that he and his wife should come to live in the flat, since at this time the Eliots had very little money.[11]

Ezra Pound, in an indulgent letter written to Wyndham Lewis in 1916, gives another reflection of Eliot's public image, Eliot "in local society" by the seashore, Eliot coming "after mature deliberation" to the conclusion that one of their acquaintances is "an ass," and Eliot walking quite by mistake into a wrong bedroom.[12] But these and other images of the external Eliot, though they may suggest something about the materials of Eliot's early poetry, offer no clue to the organization. For that we must stand with the metaphysical Eliot who is distinct from the various characters in the poems who walk streets, climb stairs, drink coffee, and brood over women. There are several ways of showing his presence. Perhaps the best way, at first, is simply to take three of Eliot's earliest and most widely read poems and show how the designs of these could not be what they are were the poet not standing on the frontier between two worlds. Such a standpoint is metaphysical, though the person occupying it need not in occupying it be a metaphysician. Eliot the metaphysician (as distinct from the metaphysical Eliot) comes later.

1909—"CONVERSATION GALANTE"

The important point to note about this poem is not that it is *vers de société* (Eliot will comment years later, rather wryly, on the facility with which critics dismiss as *vers de société* something that he meant seriously),[13] nor that it clearly shows the impact of Jules Laforgue. If we compare "Conversation Galante" with "Autre Complainte de Lord Pierrot" we see that Eliot has made something entirely different of his colloquy. Laforgue's poem is an interesting and complicated gesture, but what the gesture finally expresses is an attitude of one human being, Jules Laforgue. The moral observation implicit in the poem (for Pierrot's rejection of the poor girl is a significant moral gesture: it is a stroke in behalf of the formed against the formless, the conscious against the unconscious) is a judgment of other people, not of one's self. Eliot's procedure, fundamentally different, is that of Henry James and Nathaniel Hawthorne. He puts two persons together in order to show the presence of a third something that these two persons release by their encounter.[14]

To see what Eliot is doing, however, we have to take account of what it is that is bothering Eliot's young man in "Conversation Galante." He is untypical in that he seems to hate beauty. He is somewhat reminiscent of Matthew Arnold's lover in "Dover Beach." Both characters feel the lure of night and moonshine, and both feel obliged to point out that beauty is a bad index to the nature of reality. But here the resemblance ends. Arnold is incurious about what will happen when his skeptical lover tries to make love in a context of unbelief. Despite the famous preface calling for action in poetry, Arnold appears here to be intent on the pleasures of speechmaking. But Eliot is interested only in the action. Once the misbelieving gallant makes his stiff little overture, what then? The poem unfolds the answer. What is shown is that every word he utters misses the mark, illustrates his blindness, and at the same time implicates him in something that imposes self-recognition and leads to a point where decisive action may not be evaded. The poem is a three-round fight. Each round ends with a reversal of intention and partial recognition.

Consider, for example, Stanza 1, which is round one. What, we might ask again, is troubling the young man? It is the meaninglessness of the romantic element in life, exemplified by night, moonlight, and the girl on the terrace. These are resented because they create a craving for what does not exist. The young man, therefore, attempts to put out the eye of the moon, as it were, in order to induce (I suppose) the girl to accept a comfortable commonplace relationship where each makes use of the other for his own purposes. The girl's "How you digress!" unmasks his intention to get her to agree to be nothing, and at the same time forces up into his consciousness the fundamental mystery of his attraction to her.

Vexed by his defeat, this odd lover uses a style of speech in the second stanza that is sharp, precise, and difficult. His motive is the same. He defends unbelief; he would demonstrate that no flesh and blood response exists that anyone can make or be obliged to make to night and moonshine. He points to the artifice of art to illustrate what night and moonshine are good for and to the fact of art itself as proof of humanity's radical essential vacuity. The girl's "Does this refer to me?" like her "How you digress!" reverses his intention. He had meant to show, as Arnold does in "Dover Beach," an emptiness in the world; he is compelled to restrict his generalization to himself. Moreover, as the first stanza forced him to acknowledge something positive in himself that he had ignored, this one drives him to acknowledge something negative that he had denied. All this the girl brings about, not by design, but by being a piece in some design which works through her and yet transcends her.

By stanza three, the design that the silent observer who is the poet would have us see begins to show. The self-obsessed gallant whose "I observe," "And I then" at the beginning of each stanza has shown where the center of reality is for him, switches suddenly to "You, madam." And the matter of his discourse becomes not the fantastic, nor the aesthetic, but the metaphysical (the enemy of the absolute). Her responses, moreover, move from "you" (at the end of Stanza 1), to "me" (at the end of Stanza 2), to "we" (at the end of Stanza 3).

But the situation is still a fight, even though the young man seems to be turning gallant and seems to be paying compliments. What he speaks is approximately true. The female has twisted his sense into nonsense; she has reduced his absolutism to relativity. But his motive is the same: it is to enclose the girl in his abstract categories. Her "Are we then so serious?" brings him face to face with an "us" to which he must say yes, or no. The poem ends thus at the point where it began: with the fact of a mysterious social entity that his behavior acknowledges and his head denies. Now that entity is seen. And the young man ends where neither rhetoric, rationalization, nor ratiocination can save him. He must act. What Eliot has done in this his first "public" poem is show the presence of an Absolute in the most unpromising region of life.

1910–11—"THE LOVE SONG OF J. ALFRED PRUFROCK"

The dissociation that Eliot establishes between Prufrock's mind and the poet's mind makes this a triumph of youthful intelligence. The form of the poem (which goes far beyond "Conversation Galante") transforms a cry from hell into music. But Eliot does what he does (thus we go in a circle) because of the kind of vision that enabled F. H. Bradley to say in the "Preface" to *Appearance and Reality*, "The world is the best of all possible worlds, and everything in it is a necessary evil."

To see the organization of the poem, we may divide it into five scenes: (1) Prufrock in the streets, (2) Prufrock approaching the house, (3) Prufrock ascending the stairs to the drawing room and descending them, (4) Prufrock leaving the house, and (5) Prufrock on the beach. Scenes 1, 3, and 5 are the beginning, middle, and end of the action. Scene 1 has unusual dramatic compression; we see the protagonist between the sky and the earth taking action that misses the mark, but misses it after a fashion we are familiar with. Thus we are prepared, as in classic theatre, to watch the protagonist proceed from wrong to wrong until he or we recognize the blind spot in his motivation. Prufrock's struggle begins, of course, the moment he refuses to face the question that the streets lead him to, the question that Eliot put to himself years later in *Dry Salvages:* "Where is there an end of it?" answering: "There is no end of it."

But the middle of "Prufrock" is the climax of the poem, and here we see most clearly what the theme of this poem is; it is what some regard as the peculiar affliction of our age—metaphysical blindness.[15] Eliot's middle scene constitutes the longest and most intricate one in the poem, but if we concentrate on what is essential, following Prufrock as he struggles up the stairs, as he wrestles with the dead lumber in his head, and as he draws near to the person he has come to visit, there is a moment of suspended Prufrockian thought, a moment when Prufrock *is* his experience, a moment such as we get used to watching for in Eliot, where the door out of the corridor suddenly opens, and we are invaded by a sense of reality. The opening here is not much more than a crack: the flash of light to light as the lamplight is reflected from the brown hair on the woman's arms. But it is sufficient not only to throw Prufrock off his bent ("Is it perfume from a dress/ That makes me so digress?") but almost to bring him to act. His "Shall I say . . . ?" shows him on the verge of entering a real present. But then he falls back, and rejoins the arthropods. Why? The answer is that he has nothing to act with, just as he had nothing to confront the streets with: here, for example, he did not *see* the light answering light. This scene illustrates what is meant by the theme of metaphysical blindness.

Scene 5, Prufrock's end, his swan song, is the finest thing in the poem. Prufrock, the man to whom the mermaids will not sing, himself sings of that marvelous experience that he has been on the verge of from the beginning, that barely brushed him in the middle, and which, now, he is excluded from. His end sends us back to his beginning and suddenly the whole poem, stanza by stanza rises up as pure sound, a love song, something comic and tragic and inextinguishable. Scene 5, of course, succeeds only because of the sense of form that enabled Eliot to create that beginning and middle. But his sense of form rests on a firm metaphysical perspective which the poet never argues for, but simply takes for granted.

1910—"PORTRAIT OF A LADY."

Eliot pillaged from Laforgue again in the "Portrait," again pitted two people against one another, and again made his plot point toward a social entity that his characters affirm even when they deny. The poet seems bent on expressing a realization fundamentally terrifying, and in some respects this is the most adult and ambitious of Eliot's early efforts.[16] Eliot brings his materials so close to the reader's eyes that it is hard not to become engrossed in the materials as Conrad Aiken perhaps is in his remarks on the poem:

> Our dear deplorable friend, Miss X, the *precieuse ridicule* to end all preciosity, serving tea so exquisitely among her bric-a-brac, was to be pinned like a butterfly to a page in *Portrait of a Lady*.[17]

> Just as the oh so precious, the oh so exquisite, Madeleine, the Jamesian lady of ladies, the enchantress of the Beacon Hill drawing room—who, like another Circe, had made strange shapes of Wild Michael and the Tsetse—was afterwards to be essentialized and ridiculed (and his own pose with it) in Tsetse's *Portrait d'une Femme*.[18]

To see the poem as a design we have to back off and dissociate Eliot the poet from Eliot the man. The poet betrays his presence by the epigraph and the concluding stanza and by the patterned presentation of events between the beginning and end. The epigraph and the last stanza distance the outward action. Even though the young man's visits to the lady are given in present tense, the epigraph and the last stanza encourage us to think of this tense as a historical present—and invite us to picture the young man as re-enacting incidents of a year ago on the other side of the Atlantic, re-enacting them almost compulsively in order to revive the meaning in an experience. It is even possible to see the protagonist as offering up on a platter to a friend (the "you" in the poem) these examples of the truth of St. Augustine's re-statement of James 4:4: "The friendship of this world is fornication against Thee" (Book I, xiii, 21). Nevertheless, the fact emerges that even fornication (which must be figurative in this case, not actual) is a corruption of an immanent love.

The beginning, middle, and end of the poem are not without ambiguities. Yet we see where we are (or where the Teresias-like Eliot is) when we notice that the focus of the poet's attention is never merely the Lady nor merely the man but something between the Lady and the man which neither can get rid of nor get in tune with. Both would like, one suspects, to walk away and say "To hell with it" (Arthur Miller's expression), but they cannot. The communal entity which is the hero of Eliot's art enters here almost like the villain, transforming the Lady and her reluctant victim into *its* victims.

We sense this first in the second and third lines: "You have the scene arrange itself—as it will seem to do—/ With 'I have saved this afternoon for you.'" Here the "you" suggests the uninvolved spectator in whose presence the action is to be interpreted; and the wording of the two lines suggests how even the uninvolved spectator shall be sucked into a social situation that he knows to be false, a situation that the unlovely Lady has evoked with a cliché, a situation that once evoked rolls forward with a life of its own. Almost every word that the Lady utters in the first twenty-five lines belies a valid human association; all her word combinations are wrong—especially that having to do with the resurrection of a "soul." Yet if we consider, not what she says, but what is struggling to be born in what she says, her words are transmitted from a real reality and sometimes almost point back to it.

Without these friendships, she says, life, what *cauchemar!*
Exactly. On the other hand, when the young man finally
reacts (answering her violins and cornets with tom toms,
to have at least one definite false note; fleeing to public
places to immerse himself in a public world as spurious
as her private one) he seems to be, not a mere reflexive
action in response to her fatuity, but an expression of the
social genie that is struggling to come to consciousness
in each of them.

The middle movement of the poem (Section II) is a
series of ironic observations of the way the social genie
released by the Lady is transforming the "gulf" that separates what the Lady intends and what the young man intends into a bridge. At the climax we get a fusion of the
sundered Lady and the sundered young man when the
young man seated in the park with the comics and the
sporting page on his lap is invaded by another species of
canned music and responds by entering in idea at least
into the life of the Lady's withered heart reaching out for
a lost association. Here the Lady's previous statements
(which seemed at the time quite false) "I am always
sure . . . that across the gulf you reach your hand" become prophetic and we sense perhaps that Eliot in this
poem is up to strange things, or things strange to anyone
who had not had a course in metaphysics with Josiah
Royce.

The final movement is very complex. Drawn by guilt to
return, the young man has his candle puffed out completely by the Lady's words that deny the reality of their
association. Yet at the moment when she, like Circe,
transforms him into an animal—he, for the first time, is
human. He dances like a bear, cries like a parrot, chatters
like an ape in order to be sociable. And at the end, when
she too suffers an imaginary death, her music, her life, is
suddenly successful: the reality of the genie that has lived
between the unreality of their two lives is acknowledged
and the unreal lives become momentarily real.

To recapitulate: the metaphysical Eliot is revealed by
his concern with a social entity that exists above, beyond,

and yet within people. It is as though, for the purposes of making poetry, Eliot had taken a standpoint very much like that of Josiah Royce.

Once we are cued to Eliot's central concern, there is a second way of seeing his Teresias-like point of view. If we take the recurrent motive in the foregoing poems, it is by fairly general consent romantic yearning. Romantic yearning is love in a context of unbelief. But Eliot's presentation of this yearning is not romantic irony; it is not the pathos of human craving for what does not exist that he sees, but the irony of human mismanagement of the craving for a transcendant reality that does exist. The recurrent theme of these poems is metaphysical blindness in a world of light. Eliot could not see the comedy of these actions were he not standing at a position outside the context of unbelief. Such a position is metaphysical.

A third way to see what Eliot's standpoint is is to observe the way he uses a symbol like light, which figures in each of the six early poems. "Conversation Galante" is a moonlit poem; "Prufrock" a lamplit one; "Portrait" a candlelit; "Preludes" a street- and day-light poem; "Rhapsody" a moon and street-lamp lighted one; and "La Figlia" a sun-lighted one.

Eliot uses this light imagery very dramatically in "Preludes," "Rhapsody," and "La Figlia." In "Preludes" the world turns around a sun that is never seen—except by the prostitute in the third prelude, and by the tormented speaker in the fourth. Yet every motif in the first two preludes points to the nothingness of human beginnings and in the second two to the omnipresence of a reality infinitely gentle and infinitely suffering. This, the most obviously philosophic of the early poems, is like a variation on a text by Josiah Royce:

> But this other realm, where no fact, however slight, transient, fleeting, is absolutely independent of any of its fellow facts, this is the realm where when one member suffers others suffer also, where no sparrow falls to the ground without the insight of one who knows, and where the vine and the branches eternally flourish in sacred unity.

That is the city which hath foundations, and thither our argument already, amidst these very storms of negation, is carrying us over the waves of doubt.[19]

In "Rhapsody on a Windy Night," we have the dilemma of a protagonist whose world is lit mainly by two discordant lights. There is the moon that has lost its memory and, therefore, like the Lady in "Portrait of a Lady," can create only "a lunar synthesis," a merely aesthetic order at once romantic and unreal, evoking an appetite for an order beyond the order of quotidian life, and yet offering no light by which to find it. There are the street lamps, those representatives of contemporary consciousness (all of Eliot's lights are species of realization), and they can merely beat like fatalistic drums, repeatedly calling attention to such deterministic facts of life in the street as are visible to the most commonplace intelligence. The protagonist subjected to a long drawn-out battle with the street lamps is another victim of metaphysical blindness. He is stabbed four times between midnight and four o'clock by the light that is darkness, and the poem ends with "The last twist of the knife."

"La Figlia Che Piange" is the only poem in the group that is lighted by sunlight, and that sunlight is recollected. The protagonist re-enacts the moment when he was cut off from the body in which for him the real reality had been momentarily reflected. It is interesting the way he petitions the girl to re-reject him, but not to reject for him the reflection of a life beyond life. ("Weave, weave the sunlight in your hair.") The poem, a kind of intimations ode, ends with statements of an almost obdurate obtuseness, as if the protagonist were a mind that can respond to perceptions and respond to conceptions but not to what Josiah Royce called "interpretations." We have to recognize, however, the difference between the protagonist's view and the poet's point of view. The poet by the last two lines ("Sometimes these cogitations still amaze/ The troubled midnight and the noon's repose.") is showing that he sees that after light has answered light to light "the light is still/ At the still point of the turning world."

In case I should seem to have made too much of the fundamentally religious perspective that Eliot has embodied in his early poems, a perspective that he committed himself to as a religion only many years later, we may cite Eliot's answer to a French questioner who wondered about the often repeated idea that a break occurs between the poetry Eliot wrote before and after his religious conversion:

> JEAN DESTERNES "Le traducteur de vos poèmes, Pierre Leyris, dit que vous avez tracé une ligne de partage très nette entre vos oeuvres d'avant votre conversion au Catholicisme, et celles qui suivent?"
>
> ELIOT "Il me semble que la suivante explique la précédente, que la première est complétée et prolongée par la dernière." [20]

Conrad Aiken once remarked on the remarkable consistency of Eliot's art from beginning to end.[21] What makes it consistent is what I am calling the metaphysical basis of it. This basis is not a metaphysics—though as we shall see, Eliot moves next to a skillful formulation of his instinctive point of view. It is, in the 1910–11 poems, simply what Eliot praised in Henry James:

> His romanticism implied no defect in observation of the things he wanted to observe; it was not the romanticism of those who dream because they are too lazy or too fearful to face the fact; it issues, rather, from the imperative insistence of an ideal which tormented him. He was possessed by the vision of an ideal society; he *saw* (not fancied) the relations between the members of such a society. And no one, in the end, has ever been more aware—or with more benignity, or less bitterness—of the disparity between possibility and fact.[22]

2   THE METAPHYSICAL STANDPOINT

> "Let us not conjecture at random about the greatest things."—Heracleitus, fragment 42.

THE STRAIGHT WAY to Eliot's metaphysical standpoint is through the doctoral dissertation that he sent to Harvard in 1916, and once spoke of as unreadable. It is formidable to anyone whose interest in Eliot is merely literary. I shall attempt to approach it, first from a distance, as if it were a peak on the horizon; second from close at hand, as if we were climbers at the foot of the peak; and third from the top, describing the contents of the dissertation as though they constituted a view spread out below. The title, *Experience and the Objects of Knowledge in the Philosophy of F. H. Bradley*, fixes the standpoint to be gained. When Eliot declared that the tendency of Bradley's labours is "to bring British philosophy closer to the Greek tradition," [1] he places for us the position he wishes himself to occupy, a point where empirical and rationalistic ways of viewing the universe seem to intersect. Bradley is sometimes said to be the greatest British metaphysician after Hume.

Standing, then, first completely outside Eliot's viewpoint and viewing it from afar, we might say that Eliot takes his stand with those who make mind the key to whatever is in the universe, in contradistinction to those who choose matter. We need to add quickly, however, that to stand here does not mean, as it might seem to, to stand on the ideas that go round and round in one's brain, but to stand on what our ideas *point to*, a context of order that binds together whatever is, and makes whatever is not only what it is but "good" in its way. Similarly, to stand on one's two feet to view the world is to stand on what *bodies* point to, that multiverse where, to use Henry Adam's phrase, chaos is the rule of nature and order the dream of man.[2]

Although long-distance views of metaphysical standpoints are untrustworthy, we have to take them at first in order to get our bearings, as Eliot does in his essay on Pascal when he divides the world between those who start with certain "values" (saintliness is one of Eliot's examples) and go on to inquire what kind of a world, ultimately, must be the context of such values, and those who start with "facts" and ask: "Is a case of human parthenogenesis credible?"[3] "There are," Eliot declared in another place, "two and only two finally tenable hypotheses about life: the Catholic and the materialistic."[4] Using these terms broadly (as Eliot evidently intends) we might picture the thought of the past moving between two poles and see poets inspired by the views available from either—Lucretius who sang of the nature of things, Dante who celebrated the love that moves the planets. Both positions have provided glimpses of what Eliot once called "the horror, and the glory."[5] That no sparrow falls except for a reason is a painful as well as comforting vision, for by it man gets responsibility, which means judgment and dread. On the other hand, to think that the universe consists of infinite dice cast by nobody's hand, deprives us of hope but gives us freedom of the kind celebrated by Bertrand Russell in "A Free Man's Worship."

Sometimes Eliot's poetry expresses the horror of both world views, as well as the greater horror of holding no world view at all. But his most sombre effects come from seeing a merely materialistic universe:

> *That's all, that's all, that's all, that's all,*
> *Birth, and copulation, and death.*
> . . . . . ⸍ . . . .

> *Birth, and copulation, and death.*
> *That's all the facts when you come to*
>   *brass tacks:*
> *Birth, and copulation, and death.*[6]

ii

To pass from a long-range view of Eliot's standpoint to the standpoint itself requires something like willing suspension of disbelief.* Philosophic disbelief, however, does not suspend easily. The interpreter's position is ticklish. He approaches from below the position to be occupied, but wishes to be at the top, and so is obliged to look two ways, downward to those who deny and upward to those who affirm. What is difficult to assimilate is the element of faith in every standpoint.

Most bewildering is the way Eliot's faith seems (to those below looking up) to enable him to stand on what he has not got. He stands (like others in the tradition) on the Right Answer, which he does not know. Two quotations and an illustration may clarify the apparent scandal of his behavior. "The question is, the first question, *not* what comes natural or what comes *easy* to us, but what is right?" [7] "A man who is good for anything ought not to calculate the chance of living or dying; he ought only to consider whether in doing anything he is doing right or wrong." [8]

The first statement, from Eliot, has reference to the craft of the poet, and the second, from Socrates, has to do with the conduct of life. Neither Eliot nor Socrates professes to know what he is standing on (the Right), but both are confident that they know *of* it. Their speeches illustrate a tendency to pass over what lies in front of us (the natural, the easy, the calculable) and to stand on what seems beyond us (the Right Answer as applied to

---

* Here, in Section ii, appearances notwithstanding, the aim is not to philosophize, but to get into the open what Eliot takes for granted before he writes a word of his dissertation. Those familiar with the fundamental tenet of an idealistic philosopher should pass to Section iii where the actual description of Eliot's dissertation begins.

the aesthetic and the ethical). Another example may illustrate a leap more obviously metaphysical, Tennyson's in "Flower in the Crannied Wall,"

> *Flower in the crannied wall,*
> *I pluck you out of the crannies,*
> *I hold you here, root and all, in my hand,*
> *Little flower—but if I could understand*
> *What you are, root and all, and all in all,*
> *I should know what God and man is.*

Tennyson's statement is especially interesting because of the way Tennyson acknowledges entire ignorance of what the flower is and what God and man are, but acknowledges no ignorance whatsoever with regard to the fact of the Right Answer which covers what all three are. What does he stand on to attain such knowledge?

We could stop here and say, as Eliot does in his dissertation, that all philosophic claims rest finally on faith.[9] But such an answer strands an inquirer. So long as he remains below, discourse between the man at the top and the inquirer at the bottom is useless. Moreover, the inquirer down below is down there probably because he is skeptical of the claims put forward by the man at the top. Just because whatever is thinkable by us is thinkable only in a context of mind is no reason for asserting that whatever is must also *be* in a context of mind.[10] Or so the man below feels. He suspects that the idealistic metaphysician is guilty of intellectual arbitrariness (Eliot and Socrates refuse to face facts as *facts*) or intellectual confusion (people like Eliot and Socrates are seduced by false analogies). And Tennyson, confronted by

Flower plus crannied wall plus poet equals what?

exemplifies both confusions. Either the Victorian poet has not observed that flowers and crannied walls do not add up, or he has confused his present situation with one in the schoolroom where confronted by the problem "two plus three plus four equals—?" he knew that he did not know the right answer but knew that there was one.

What, in the last three lines, is Tennyson standing upon when he makes his enormous claim that a tie binds all things to all things? Poetic inspiration? So it seems to the inquirer to whom Eliot speaks as he once did in Josiah Royce's seminar: "To understand my point of view, you have to believe it first." [11] Let us see, however, if we can assume a belief that places us at Eliot's standpoint.

The question separating those below and those above is: How can a thinking person reason about the world from the standpoint of an unknown but assumed Right Answer? But this question arises (now let us begin to leap toward Eliot's standpoint) from a failure of imagination.

Another brief reference to Tennyson may introduce the kind of dramatic situation from which, perhaps, metaphysics springs. Tennyson once spoke of "nature" as "red in tooth and claw." (*In Memoriam*, LV.) This interesting expression suggests a Victorian who does not know where to stand, his eyes having been opened by science to the unethical character of the natural and the unnatural character of the ethical. He migrates between two worlds unable to be a resident of either. He needs a metaphysician, but does not know it yet. When John Keats (whose intuitions were remarkable) wrote that a quarrel in the streets is a hateful thing though the energies displayed are fine,[12] he was offering Tennyson a standpoint where conflicts of ethical and natural seem to sink in a third order. Aestheticism is the solution that, according to Eliot,[13] Matthew Arnold offered the Victorian world, when he offered literature as a "consolation and stay." [14] But if, now, attending to Baudelaire's experience, we answer Keats, for Tennyson, that though the spectacle of a quarrel in the streets is a horrible thing, the spectacle of an *hypocrite lecteur* [15] responding aesthetically to a quarrel in the streets is a more horrible thing, we shall have brought Tennyson to the crisis from which a metaphysician must rescue him. He roves between three worlds, torn between three points of view, and rests in none. If metaphysics is, in Eliot's definition, the effort to "bind" all points of view into one point of view,[16] or, the study of *the* viewpoint,[17] Tennyson needs metaphysics.

Yet when Eliot speaks of metaphysics as the attempt to "bind" all points of view into one point of view, he uses language of this world and employs a metaphor that seems to preclude success. If naturalistic, ethical, and aesthetic points of view are fixed in independent standpoints, no effort can "bind" them. On the other hand, when he speaks of metaphysics as the study of *the* viewpoint, he uses appropriate metaphysical language but precludes communication with the world. To grasp what can and cannot be done for one like Tennyson, we need, despite the difficulties of communication, to take up the second definition and examine the idea of a "science" of point of view.

No term in Eliot's dissertation (with the possible exception of "object") is more important than "point of view." It has a precise place in a system of concepts; but, in the end, the whole dissertation is a definition of "point of view." Here it will suffice, perhaps, to mark out some obvious meanings of the familiar phrase. "Point of view" would seem to me (though Eliot does not say so) to involve four factors, and a gardener's maze may illustrate them.[18] There are bushes, a network of paths, the center of the maze, and a bewildered visitor. The center is the point in the point of view, the paths are the view, the bushes are seemingly chaotic facts of experience, and the visitor is the quester after knowledge. Eliot's use of the term "point of view" has a wide range of reference and nothing on earth would seem to be more prevalent. Every moment of attention is a point of view. A thirsty tiger that quits his lair to find a water hole has a point of view. Children counting television antennae on a long automobile ride have found a point of view to organize their experiences. Sir Isaac Newton formulating the law of gravitation is fixing a point of view.

The differences between having, finding, and fixing a point of view may introduce a difference between scientific "knowing" and metaphysical "knowing." In principle the difference is simple. Scientific knowing is *view*-oriented. Metaphysical "knowing" is standpoint-oriented. It is customary to say that science is concerned with questions of fact, philosophy with questions of meaning. But in terms of the metaphor of the maze, may we say that science is concerned with *fixing a* standpoint? But the metaphysician is concerned to know *the* standpoint, an entirely different effort.

In fixing a standpoint, the scientist does not have to know what he is standing on (any more than does the tiger, or the children.) What he knows is that there is a "view" and that he knows the formula for seeing it. Moreover, he is not *having* that standpoint when he is *fixing a* standpoint. The traveller, for example, photographing his own footsteps, is not at the moment of clicking the camera shutter standing in those footprints. But he is doing something such as the scientist does; he is fixing where he has stood. For this reason, the scientist having made many fixes of his standpoints encourages us to speak of standpoints (plural). But if we stick to the experience of *having* the standpoint (which of course we cannot do, because as soon as we look at our feet we are no longer standing in *those* shoes), or if we keep in mind whatever it is that enables us to distinguish *having* and *fixing*, we will be inclined to speak of *the* standpoint, as we have in speaking of metaphysics as the study of *the* standpoint.

The paradox of metaphysical inquiry may now be clear. We cannot "know" the standpoint, since knowing, for us, means making where we have stood part of a view, and the standpoint is never part of a view while we are *having* it.[19] The task of the metaphysician, from the outside, must seem endless and futile since he can never *have* what he is in pursuit of, and yet he always has it, or it has him.

But, the activity of the metaphysician can not be understood from without. When, like Tennyson, we are caught in a metaphysical problem and *need* the metaphysician, we understand him. For our disease demands, not knowledge of a standpoint, but *acknowledgment* of it. What the metaphysician can do is show a Tennyson that his being *on* the roads between worlds *is* the standpoint. This incapacity to live ultimately either in the natural or the ethical or the aesthetic worlds is a symptom of *the* standpoint. Tennyson has unconsciously identified *the* standpoint with fixations of the standpoint—the scientific and the ethical. But the standpoint will not be *fixed* or known. It will be known of, or acknowledged, and will stir up trouble until it is.

The kind of acknowledgment that the metaphysician seeks is not easy to give because it requires a reversal of normal habits of knowing, which are view-oriented instead of standpoint-oriented. The acknowledgment requires a kind of sensibility more characteristic of artists, perhaps, than of practical men of affairs, though I say this, not because I am sure it is so, but as a way of returning to the problem of what the metaphysician is standing on when *he* is doing his job. For those outside the metaphysical predicament (which is to say, inside some physical problem requiring the services of a scientist) the metaphysician seems to be standing on nothing. Let us reexamine "two plus three plus four equals—?" and "flower plus crannied wall plus poet equals—?" Let us make a distinction between the kind of sensibility that responds to the background of a situation and the kind that responds to the foreground. The charge has been made that Socrates and Eliot and Tennyson, in taking a stand on the Right Answer, are standing on what they have not got, on what is not "given." But the answer that we now might give is that the Right Answer is the only element in the situation that *is* given, that is *there* beyond doubt.[20] It is given as background, not foreground. The way to see it is to concentrate on the symbol of the question mark, the most significant symbol among the six signs. To see the significance, however, we must believe that every symbol participates in the being of what it stands for, and we must be able, like literary critics (rather than like good mathematicians) to take the question mark as a character in a dramatic situation. Then we might say, perverse as it might sound to a mathematician, that the question mark *is* what it denotes, in the sense that Tennyson's on-the-road outcast state is the ultimate standpoint (unrecognized). What the question mark designates is the right answer; but what question mark *is* as question mark *is* the Right Answer. It *is* the background of the situation, it is the kind of "minding" that makes the arithmetical signs *signs* and not ink blots on the page, it is that felt background of order that Tennyson feels in writing his poem and which, if he did not feel, the brute facts of flower and wall, etc. would not be brute facts.

I am arguing, it would seem, that the metaphysician taking his stand on the Right Answer is our only real *empiricist* because he starts from being in a situation (foreground and background, view and viewpoint) whereas the scientist starts from where he has been (foreground, only), which is to say, with "facts" abstracted from the situation as given. Perhaps this is why F. H. Bradley argues that metaphysical truths are the only truths we possess that are incorrigible.[21]

To accept metaphysics as the acknowledgment of the standpoint is to cease to resist some of the inversions of classical metaphysics. It is disconcerting when Plato dismisses the material table as "appearance," and refers to another world where the immutable, eternal, and invisible "real" table is. It is more disconcerting when F. H. Bradley reduces to "appearance" everything that seems to make existence "real"—things, selves, space, time, even "truth" itself—and departs with the assurance that all appearances are made real in the Absolute, just how, he cannot say.

But through the by-now symbolic "two plus three plus four equals—?" we may be enabled to see that "appearance" and "reality" are but names for the left hand and right hand symbols, for view and standpoint, and that what ultimately disturbs us is the feeling that the names metaphysicians favor for the characters in their metaphysical drama are ill-chosen. Dramatistically they are well-chosen. The integers on the left *appear*; they are the *appearance* of the background of order called the Right Answer, in the sense that a great actor's public appearance now in this role and now in that are expressions of what otherwise could not be realized. The great actor is not his public appearances but he would not be himself without his appearances. So "two plus three plus four" is not the Right Answer (nor is the number 9) yet the Reality is in the appearance without being it. Likewise to make what the question mark denotes "Reality" is also good dramatistically. As has been said, the question mark is the mode of minding without which the numbers would be ink blots. The question mark points to the gold bullion that makes paper money real money and not paper. What could be more appropriate than to call that which makes appearance real the principle of Reality?

Once we acquire the metaphysician's peculiar sensibility, though, we may run to an opposite extreme and say, How easy! Anyone can be a metaphysician! Eliot's tribute to F. H. Bradley speaks of the bewildered despair such a philosopher induces, where you wonder "why you ever wanted anything, and what it was you wanted, since this philosophy seems to give you everything you ask and yet to render it not worth wanting." [22]

But, actually, a metaphysician leads a laborious life. His labours are never done. The reason is that people will think, and thinking mostly means *fixing* a viewpoint, and sooner or later *the* standpoint gets fixed in a view. Man is said to be a metaphysical animal. Consciously or unconsciously he will absolutize his views. So appears the metaphysician *manqué* who either makes the physical metaphysical or the metaphysical physical. The labour of the classic metaphysician is always the same, to reaffirm the Right Answer by unfixing it from every answer.

A familiar example will illustrate the strategy. Early in the discussion of what justice is, in Plato's *Republic*, Thrasymachus declares that justice is whatever the strong want to do.[23] His declaration is that of a man of the world impatient to rescue the discussion from academic abstractions. His realism consists of asserting the independence of what the ruler wants from what the ruled want. Socrates' response diverts attention from what Thrasymachus thinks to where Thrasymachus lives, a context of order where the governor and governed are mutually involved. So Socrates affirms the omnipresent Right Answer, which cannot speak, but must be acknowledged.

F. H. Bradley re-employed the strategy in three works that established his reputation: *Ethical Studies*, 1876, *Principles of Logic*, 1883, and *Appearance and Reality*, 1893.[24] Confronting a hedonistic ethics (good behaviour is what aggregates the greatest quantity of pleasure for the greatest number), an associationist logic (the truth of any judgment rests on the fact that two unwedded ideas have appeared in public so long together that every one regards them as married), and a skeptical metaphysics (since all we know is a storm of sensations, what certitude have we that the spatter exemplifies any order, or comes from an outer world? Or what likelihood is there that you registering sensations from there and I from here can register anything that adds up to the totality of things?), confronting these outlooks Bradley demanded, like Socrates, that experience be re-examined as it is, and that all the facts of ethical, logical, or metaphysical situations be examined. As a result he found, in *Ethical Studies*, that the atoms of pleasure tallied by utilitarians are abstractions and that what we really have is an actor embedded in a context of social order.[25] This context (the community in which I live and which assigns me my station and duties) determines right and wrong conduct. In *Principles of Logic* he found (when he looked at thinking as it is, not as it is thought to be) judgment embedded in a context of order containing the thinker.[26] (This context is the Absolute, the real subject of every predicate. To say, "Grass is green" is not to make a statement about my sensibility, but to make a statement about the universe. It is to say that the world is such that at my focus of vision grass *has* to be green.) In *Appearance and Reality* he found not only himself but the skeptical embedded in an ultimate context of order which the skeptic inadvertently appealed to in the very act of asserting that we know nothing beyond our experience.[27] When he examined the realist's "realities," he found the thingiest of things reacting violently against the suggestion that they are anything but appearance. Like children proud to present the school play these things gesture perpetually toward a world which they themselves cannot see and which we cannot see, but which we must assume to be the real reality if we are to make any kind of sense at all of our behaviour or the behaviour of things. To this tradition in metaphysics Eliot gave himself.

iii

We pass now to the third stage of this essay. When Eliot, at the end of his dissertation, declares that there are no novelties in the fundamentals of philosophy, only an ever more rigorous working out of details,[28] he is implying, I believe, that standpoints in philosophy are limited and ancient, but landscapes unlimited and always new. The view, therefore, has to be rediscovered in every age. We move now with Eliot to an old standpoint, and try to follow the involutions of a complicated contemporary landscape, or a landscape that was contemporary in 1916. Three terms in the title of Eliot's dissertation mark out three directions we must look if we are to follow Eliot. They are "[I] *Experience* and [II] the *Objects* of [III] *Knowledge* in the Philosophy of F. H. Bradley." To keep these terms distinct while keeping them conjoined, let us arbitrarily employ Shelley's image of "life like a dome of glass" to illustrate the I, the II and the III, recognizing all the while how untrustworthy any concrete image must be in philosophical discourse. Shelley's lines run as follows:

> *Life, like a dome of many-colored glass,*
> *Stains the white radiance of Eternity,*
> *Until Death tramples it to fragments.*

Shelley's radiance is the real, what Eliot's "experience" points to; the glass is the ideal, what Eliot's "knowledge" points to; the stain is appearance, what Eliot's "objects" are. But radiance, glass, and stain, though distinguishable are not separable.

Using Shelley's image as a globe, we may chart Eliot's strategy. Chapter I, "Of Our Knowledge of Immediate Experience" has the *radiance* as the point of attention; Chapter II, "Of the Distinction Between Real and Ideal" has the *dome of glass*; Chapter III, "The Psychologist's Treatment of Knowledge," and Chapters IV and V, "The Epistemologist's Treatment of Knowledge" have types of *stains* (types of objects) under observation. (Eliot picks off the "half objects"—mental presentations, mental contents—of the introspective psychologist, and the "real" objects—physical things—and "unreal" objects—chimerical things—of the realistic philosophers.) Chapter VI, "Solipsism" has the point of intersection of radiance and glass as the point to be surveyed. (As his chapter title indicates, the difficulty is a mistake about the point of view, a confusion of the real subject with the self and the soul.) Chapter VII, "The Conclusion" is hard to chart. It is about the dome of glass so irradiated with radiance by a point that the stain is like radiance. It is about metaphysical knowledge.

As is obvious, Eliot's trip around the dome of glass is a campaign. The enemy is the metaphysician *manqué*. In Chapters I and II, he is internal to Eliot himself, the treacherous "thinker" who loses the standpoint by fixing it in a view, either by (here I have to mix metaphors) transforming radiance into stain or glass into stain. Chapters I and II are important, therefore, because they free the standpoint. In Chapter III, the enemy is the introspective psychologist (now extinct, I suppose,) who launches himself feet first at the essentially metaphysical (mental "fact") as if it were physical. In Chapters IV and V, the enemy is at the opposite pole, the realistic metaphysician like Bertrand Russell who converts the physical into the metaphysical by *fiat*. In Chapter VI, the enemy is internal again, the "thinker" who looks at the standpoint as a "thing" and sees neither radiance nor glass but a point of flicker. Chapter VII is, of course, the triumphal procession.

Anyone who reads Eliot's dissertation at this date must speculate about the state of mind and motives of the writer. My advance description must inevitably give a misleading impression of these. The tone, for example, seems to me similar to that at the close of *The Waste Land*: Shall I at least set my lands in order? Eliot seems convinced of what his dissertation discloses, but seems also to find the conclusions somewhat hard, like the old man in "The Journey of the Magi." But my speculations seem irrelevant to the content of the dissertation, which I shall try now to translate into terms of my own. Since Eliot does not permit quotation, the result is bound to be somewhat embarrassing, like a translation of Kant into Chinese pictographs. But Eliot's restriction has the merit of forcing us to try to picture the dissertation as a whole.

Chapter I, "Of Our Knowledge of Immediate Experience" is an inquiry, then, about Shelley's white radiance, or—it comes to the same thing—an effort to focus the real at the point where it touches a standpoint. The inquiry is embarrassed by the fact that nothing can be known about immediate experience as such. To know in our terms is to objectify and when immediate experience is so fixed, so objectified it is no longer immediate experience. Yet, as Bradley pointed out,[29] the recognition of immediate experience is a matter of utmost importance: such acknowledgment is the way to the solution of ultimate problems. Eliot's solution to the dilemma is to show that we are compelled to acknowledge immediate experience, though we can have no knowledge about it. By focusing situations now from the side of feeling and now from the side of thought we can show that it is a necessary inference.

Suppose (and whatever illustrations are introduced hereafter are my own and neither Eliot nor F. H. Bradley should shoulder the responsibility), suppose in an unfamiliar room, a sleeper wakes up and confronts utter darkness. "*What* is *this?*" he cries. "What" and "this" show the two sides of the situation. *This* points to the felt foundation of the situation and hence is a verbal arrow pointing toward immediate experience. "What" points to where thought is busy trying to set up some identifying relationships. If we imagine the sleeper trying to focus his thoughts and not succeeding, we may be tempted to say that the situation consists of *thisness* and nothing but thisness (no *whatness*) and here, therefore, *is* immediate experience. But Eliot firmly rejects the view that we ever have immediate experience as *an* experience. Here, for the befuddled sleeper, the whatness may not be high-grade or prominent, but it is there. "*What* is *this?*" implies attention and attention implies a point of attention and a point of attention implies an "object" of knowledge, however low grade. The utter darkness is "black space" (an object) or "bad moment" (another object) for an *object* does not have to be physical to be an object. Any *this-what* will do.

Keeping the half-awakened sleeper still in mind, we may be tempted, nevertheless, to think that the farther we are from having our wits about us the closer we are to immediate experience. Nothing could be more wrong. Immediate experience (it *is* the point in the standpoint) is omnipresent, as much present in the mathematician's abstract meditations as in erotic ecstasy, even though as Bradley allows, to find reality we must betake ourselves to feeling.[30] Yet to know of it, which is the business of Eliot's chapter, we must focus a situation now *this*-ward and now *what*-ward.

If after crying, "What is this?" the sleeper suddenly recalls driving at sundown into some city, and registering at some hotel, he may suddenly cry, "Ah, *this* is Chicago; *this* is my room at the Conrad Hilton." "Black space" is now "dark room" and there is a "me" confronting it. But "thisness" has not departed; it remains in the situation the lurking critic of conclusive conclusions. Suppose the sleeper re-examines "this" and says: "That was last week. What is *this?*" Instantly the objective room collapses and thought must begin again.

To see the limitations of such terms as "subjective" and "objective" is to be driven to examine the background of our lives where knowing begins. What Eliot thinks he can safely say about *this* may now be summarized.

First, "this" is the foundation and goal of all our knowing.[31] (Thought starts with *this*, and the act of thought merely points to other manifestations of this.) *This* is the one independent reality.[32] (Hotel rooms are carved out of *this*, and selves that sleep in hotel rooms are too.) *This* is the criterion of our judgments.[33] (What makes a situation "real," and not just something thought up, is the affinity of *this* for the situation. The moment *this* withdraws, the situation is "unreal.") *This* is the subject of all predicates.[34] (*This* is dark; *this* is silent; *this* is a hotel room; *this* is Chicago.) *This*, we can say, finally, is the way the real comes to us, as immediate experience which we cannot know, because knowledge transforms it into appearance, but which we can know of by necessary inference.[35]

Eliot, then, in the first chapter, attempts to clarify *immediate experience*, the concept which, Bradley insisted, opens the one road to the solution of ultimate problems. What the phrase designates is something so simple that we are bound to have trouble with it. To identify "reality" with whatever it is that "immediate experience" designates is to stand Plato on his head and to identify being with Plato's non-being.

Two statements in the first chapter deserve comment. It is inevitable, Eliot says, that objects should seem to have a public character and feelings a private one.[36] The hotel room, for example, seems to be "out there," whereas the half-awakened sleeper's anxious emotions are "in here." But, Eliot declares, our emotions are no more subjective than is light because the blind cannot see it. Anger and fear affect the blood stream, influence bodily behaviour, and may be better understood by an outside observer than by ourselves.[37] Emotions, it would seem, are part of a situation: their thisness is indissociable from their whatness. The fact that they have to be felt before they can be said to exist can be said of a table, or any other object. Eliot here explicates a thought from *Appearance and Reality* which he will quote in the notes to *The Waste Land* six years later.[38]

The second statement has to do with the determination of objects of experience. We find Eliot affirming that whatever objects appear in a finite center are determined by their context.[39] I construe this to mean that *what* the white radiance appears as is determined by where on the dome of glass it strikes. Eliot goes on to say that this determination is unending. I interpret as follows: Had the body of the hotel room occupant been feverish, the objects would have been different; had he been a shell-shocked soldier, they would have been different; had he not remembered coming to Chicago, his objects would have been quite different. This insight, which seems quite commonplace, is nevertheless important. Eliot's rationalism and conservatism—his royalism, catholicism, classicism—are rooted in his ontology.

Chapter II, "Of the Distinction of Real and Ideal," presents the same dilemma as Chapter I. Eliot is obliged to ask: "What is the dome of glass?" and equally obliged to declare that no answer can be given. Thought (i.e., the ideal element in experience) cannot be an object of thought. Nevertheless, Eliot is not silenced. By careful focusing of appearances, he attempts to say what the whatness is *not*, and so lead to inferences of what it is.

When the man in the hotel room said, "What is this?", and then said, "This is a hotel room," the indeterminate became determinate, the seemingly subjective became seemingly objective. Such experiences might encourage us to conclude that half the reality of any situation consists of its ideality. When we race at eighty miles an hour down a familiar highway, the sensation of green blur is not green blur but *forest* by virtue of the knowledge that we bring to the mere feeling. Idea-ing (thinking is idea-ing for Eliot) therefore is an omnipresent accompaniment to feeling, and for Bradley there is no more serious error than that of thinking that feeling and thought are separable.[40] Yet they are distinguishable and having distinguished that element in experience which is the significance of the experience, what may be said of it? What is idea-ing? Eliot takes a long time to answer this question, and when he has finished, he confesses that his account of "idea" does not coincide with that of any other author with whom he is acquainted.[41]

The gist of Eliot's answer is as follows: an idea is "meaning" or "intention." The idea is that which intends and the real is that which is intended.[42] This at any rate is what he says. But might we put it another way? Might we say that the "idea" is an act of pointing, and the real is what is pointed to? I think so. And by so doing we see that "idea-ing" is essentially pure act. It is a "betweenness-ing" and quite transparent. It has no more self-existence than a pointing has apart from the finger which points and the object pointed to. As a consequence, it becomes easily confused with the *this* from which it takes off, and the this at which it comes to rest. These mistaken identifications are bad only when exclusive, for though the idea *is* essentially a pointing, it is, nonetheless, *also* the pointer and the pointed to, although it is these not as idea-as-such but as idea-as-world-process. (Eliot does not make the point quite this way; he suggests merely that under investigation the ideal turns out to be the real and the real the ideal, that these are but two aspects of a continuous process.[43]) At stage one of the process (as I see it), the idea is the psychological idea—the idea as datum; at stage two, the idea is the idea as act; at stage three, it is the idea as an act completed, the idea as it appears in a completed judgment: This is a hotel room. A fourth stage evidently occurs when the act itself is contemplated and behind that act a controlling grid of necessity is dimly discerned. That grid of necessity, taken as a kind of fatality in which the act of pointing is involved, is (I think) what Eliot means by the idea-as-concept.

The most significant (I find) and most difficult part of the chapter occurs when Eliot seeks to distinguish the idea as it is in judgment from the idea as concept.[44] Judgment, Eliot states, occurs whenever there is the appreciation of a givenness and the relation of it to the subject's world. A sea anemone (Eliot's illustration) which accepts or rejects a proffered morsel (we are reminded of the old crab in "Rhapsody on a Windy Night" that grasps a stick that the poet extends to him) is making a judgment.[45]

But the concept is harder to get at. Eliot uses paradoxical language to speak of it. Concepts, he declares, are omnipresent; we apprehend them intuitively, but not a single concept can be said to be known by us. Concepts are ideal; in another sense they are the only realities. The development of language is a history of the exploration of concepts; properly speaking, nevertheless, they can never be defined at all. We speak of them only in a sense. Reality exists only through its appearances (*objects* of knowledge). But concepts exist only in *ideas*. The pointing of the ideas at the concepts constitutes the reality of the concepts. An idea is that which a word refers to in actuality; a concept is that which a word denotes. Thus Eliot speaks of the concepts.[46]

Eliot's attitude toward the concepts seems to me to hypostatize them until they become mysterious and beautiful, like Platonic presences. Perhaps (I am not confident that this is true) we can comprehend by reducing the reference to very simple things. For example: I am using the idea of "edible" in a judgment the moment I recognize edible morsels before I eat them. But to have knowledge of the concept "edibility" I would have to know what I am in the scheme of things and what things are edible to such a creature as I and why and where and how they are edible. My ignorance in this regard is like Tennyson's before the flower in the crannied wall. For me to point is easy; I do so continuously. But for me to take account of (1) the pointed, (2) the pointing, (3) the pointed to (which turns out to be another network of pointings) is to confront a mystery. The idea like a neon-arrow darts back and forth between radiance and darkness. The concept is the total fatality which guides the arrow from this point to that. To have knowledge of that fatality would be to comprehend the organization of the dome of glass in one illumination. We would have to comprehend the totality of pointing implied in a single act of pointing. Does Eliot's concept of the concept not turn out to be the Absolute as Idea (the dome of glass) and the counterpart of the Absolute as Real (the white radiance of eternity)?

Chapters III, IV, and V turn from the real and ideal as such to objects as objects. Characteristically, Eliot tends to show first what objects are *not* in order to show what they are. He takes certain "objects" which some men think are "objects" and argues that they are nonobjects (though he courteously calls them half-objects). Then he takes up certain objects which some men call real objects and attempts to show that these do not differ objectwise from those they call unreal. These discussions culminate in explications of "fact" and "material world." The chapters involve polemics directed toward certain psychologists (like Stout) and neorealistic philosophers like Bertrand Russell and Meinong. The polemics I shall ignore. Eliot's view on the objectivity of objects is what is of interest.

Chapter III, "The Psychologist's Interpretation of Knowledge" raises the question whether mental things ("mind," "consciousness," "mental experience," "ideas") can be objects in the same sense that things not mental are (stone, blood vessels, etc.) Eliot concludes that the "half objects" of analytical psychology are not objects of science.[47] I shall not reproduce his arguments since the conclusion possibly merely makes explicit what was implicit in his first two chapters. Once we assume that whatever is is in a context of mind; once we assume that the world is a whole whose stuff is feeling and whose structure is thought, have we not discarded the possibility of a separate science of mind? An investigation of what experience really is is metaphysics; and an investigation of what thought really is is logic. I think we see why Eliot calls the data of the analytical psychologist "half objects." They are *this*-whats or this-*whats*; they are not *this-whats*.

What is new and interesting in Chapter III is Eliot's tentative definition of scientific fact. (Or this is what is interesting to the person who approaches the dissertation remembering Eliot's statement in "Function of Criticism" that what distinguishes the great literary critic is a highly developed sense of fact, together with his evasive conclusion that to define "sense of fact" was not his purpose in that essay.)

A scientific fact (to come to the hub of Eliot's discussion at once) is not merely a recognizable object, but an object recognized and certified to be in a specifiable field of vision.[48] "Grass is green," would not (if I follow Eliot) be a statement of fact. "To me, grass is green," would be. The principle is, apparently, that grass is green only at specific points on the dome of glass. Where my dog is, grass is not green. Where I am, it is. Thus for an object to be a scientific object, we must not only place the object, but place the placement of it.

We encounter here once again Eliot's preoccupation with the world of concepts. A sea anemone, I infer, can pass judgment on things edible and inedible, but not possess a science until it attains some awareness of membership in a community of sea anemones. At least some such consideration as this evidently underlies Eliot's declaration that facts are not merely found in the world and then laid out like bricks.[49] Every fact has a place prepared for it in the world before it ever arrives. Were there not such a pre-existent system in which fact belongs, the fact would not be a fact at all. So, Eliot goes on to say, there is a sense in which every science is a priori: the basic point of view of the science exists before the science exists, and the development of a science is organic rather than mechanical. It moves by a rejection and selection of facts that are coherent with a single point of view. What Eliot here means by "single point of view" might again be illustrated by the sea anemone's approach to life. What it sees is determined by what it is, a creature with such and such organs face to face with such a world as a creature with such and such organs is bound to have.

But—to return to that which provoked these distinctions—the science of the mind (as conceived by psychologists like Stout) is no science because it has no factual object to start with.[50] When it concerns itself with "this," it is metaphysics; when it concerns itself with "what," it is logic; insofar as it deals with "this-whats," it is one of the other sciences, probably biology.

Chapters IV and V of Eliot's dissertation, both titled "The Epistemological Theory of Knowledge," treat the problem of objects "real" and "unreal." The United States Capitol would be an example of the first; the disconsolate chimera of the second. Almost everyone recognizes a difference. The question is: What is the difference? Is it simply that the Capitol, as Bertrand Russell would tell us, is both inside my head and outside in the world, whereas the disconsolate chimera is exclusively inside my head? Eliot says no.

Eliot's objections to Russell's explanations seem to be of two sorts.[51] His first is that Russell would not know that the chimera is chimerical had he not, long before encountering it, already divided his world into real and unreal. For him subsequently to declare that the chimericalness of the chimera obliges him to postulate a mind apart as its lair does not explain how in the first place he separated his mental constituents into chimerical and nonchimerical. Eliot's second objection is that Russell having parted the world into mind and not-mind is powerless to explain how things like the United States Capitol make the leap and reside in two worlds at once.[52] He feels that the step Russell has taken to preserve the reality of a real world dissolves that reality. Thus Eliot's chapter can be thought of as falling into two halves. In the first he tries to show what the nature of Russell's "real" world is. In the second he seeks to show the nest of difficulties that we thrust ourselves into when we divide the world into the absolutely real and unreal, instead of resting content with the insight that every situation is partly real and partly unreal and that degrees of reality are the most we can hope to detect. The first part of the chapter, with Eliot's explication of Russell's "real world" is what interests me.

Suppose (and once again I must resort to a simple illustration of my own) in sorting alphabetized cards I find a "z" card that follows a "c" card. Here, I say, is a mistake. Suppose I find a card that has no identification at all, that is not even the same size, color, or composition. "What is this?" I ask. "That is nothing," somebody answers. "Throw it away." The first card typifies an erroneous object. The second (I believe) a chimerical or hallucinatory one. An object that does not occupy the position that it ought in a system that I am attending to is an erroneous object; an object that does not occupy any position in any system that I am interested in is chimerical. Whatever ploy I am making in life makes me (like the sea anemone) sensitive to the order whereby I discard the "z" card as out of place, and the null card as null. This order, which is quite ideal, constitutes a "world." Suppose while hunting, I see something fly across the sky and say, "At last, a duck!" then, lowering my piece, say, "No, just a gnat." From Eliot's lofty metaphysical perspective, the object I called "duck" is, as object, as objective as the object I subsequently called "gnat." [53] The "duck" is a mistake, but the mistake does not alter the objectivity of the "duck." (It is a this-what and so is the gnat.) The significant difference is that the this-what which I call "gnat" is more consistent with a "world," and this is a matter, not of the existence or objectiveness of objects, but of their degrees of reality, degrees of reality attained through coherence with a world. Because I am hunting, the gnat has a greater degree of reality than the "duck"; but were I attempting to refute Bertrand Russell, as Eliot is, their status in a metaphysical system must be the same, and I would concur in the judgment that whatever object succeeds in appearing to us must exist somewhere and somehow and must necessarily be a member of some world even though it be a pink elephant.

We are ready now for the significant question: What is the status of that "world" which Bertrand Russell absolutizes as "real"? Is it the really real world? Is there an absolute difference between the United States Capitol and Shakespeare's Hamlet? Eliot's answer [54] to the last question is that the "reality" of the United States Capitol consists of its membership in a system of objects that includes my body, a membership which Hamlet has not got. His answer to the first question is that that world, being the sphere of practical activity, is of crucial interest to every body; but, he goes on to declare, to say that this is *the* world, or that an admission card to the world of physical things is an adequate criterion of an object's ultimate reality is to fly in the face of experience and assert the thing that is not. Eliot does not state the matter in quite these words, but this is in essence the gist of his very Bradleian reply to Russell's realism. We would not misrepresent the spirit of his answers were we to say that in the context of our ultimate concern (our concern to *be*) the United States Capitol and Shakespeare's Hamlet have exactly the same status; they are both objects of concern, only Shakespeare's Hamlet concerns us a little more ultimately than the mere physique of the United States Capitol.

What makes Eliot's destructive analysis of Russell's "real" world interesting is the constructive view of "world" that he manages to make emerge from it. Why does the corporeal world seem so real to us that we try to make it "the one real world"? We do because of the strength of our ultimate concern. (Again, I am formulating this first in my own terms, then in Eliot's.) Reality, Eliot declares, as it comes to us (immediate experience) contains unresolvable contradictions.[55] We struggle to resolve those contradictions, for our lot is, not to contemplate a harmonious universe, but to struggle to contemplate one. Our conviction, as we struggle, is that somewhere an order does exist which will contain and resolve all contradictions of our experience. We struggle toward *that* order, and the form our struggle takes is the creation of worlds. To create a world is to find a field of vision wherein all the objects envisioned are objects of one type. In simple terms, this means that what the sea anemone struggles toward is the comforting assurance that what is focused here as edible will be focused elsewhere as contented digestion, and what I focus here as wild duck will still be wild duck from over there (in another finite centre of perception) the next moment when I get my gun to my shoulder and pull the trigger. Whether "over there" means "me experiencing this wild duck two hours from now when I proudly exhibit my prowess to my companions," or "you focusing this wild duck right now from a point of vantage" is unimportant. Each (yours or mine) is equally a new finite center of perception. Thus, Eliot declares, the objectivity of the object is the least consequential thing about it.[56] Any point of attention is an object. What is significant is from how many points of view (i.e.—in how many finite centers) the point of attention is cognizable as the same point of attention.

What then is the "real" world which Russell makes the real real world? It is, Eliot decides, an indefinite world of identical references, especially the identical references of the civilized adults that we come in contact with.[57] The system of objects coextensive with my body for me and your body for you becomes one of the most coherent and orderly and precisely defined that we can know. Motivated by the need to find a world in which we can rest from contradiction, we try to believe that this well-defined world is the only really real one. But to absolutize the physical world thus is to mistake a single zone on Shelley's dome of glass for the whole dome, or (to put the matter another way) it is to confuse a partial and practical point of view with a total or metaphysical one.[58] This is the error, Eliot feels, that Russell has made.

This insight into the ideality of our worlds which Eliot takes from Bradley is a permanent influence in his thinking. We find for example that his criticism of literary realism rests on it, as does his comparison of the world of Ben Jonson and the world of Shakespeare. His criticism of Tennyson as one thoroughly assimilated to his world (and therefore incapable of real thinking or artistic crea-

tion that has finality) rests on the perception that the
world that our practical perspective projects is constantly
taking us captive. As a matter of fact, *The Waste Land*
could be looked upon as a study of the cultural disintegra-
tion that follows the loss of a metaphysical point of view.

Chapter V of Eliot's dissertation is coordinate with
the preceding one. Whereas Chapter IV seeks to show
that objects real from a practical point of view have but
partial reality from a metaphysical point of view, Chapter V reveals that those objects that seem unreal from a
physicalistic standpoint are just objects from an ultimate
perspective. The problem of the chapter: What kind of
existence do unreal objects have? is a factitious one for
Eliot, a problem that we create for ourselves the moment
we arbitrarily identify reality with the physical world.[59]
This factitious question nevertheless elicits forty pages of
discussion in Eliot's manuscript. What is the purpose of
so much discussion? Perhaps to add the strokes to complete the picture of objects. Nevertheless, the conclusion
is that there is really very little to say about objects as
objects.[60] "This" we have always with us, and "what" we
have always with us, so that at every moment of our wak-
ing lives, objects of some kind confront us, even though
their degree of reality may be so low that we ignore them.
It is not possible, Eliot concludes, to make an exact description of the relation between real and unreal.[61] Every
time we make a judgment, like, "This is a hotel room,"
we are drawing a distinction between a "real" world in
which we are placing an experience and an "unreal" one
from which we are excluding it. But, he says, we do not
ourselves know these worlds. We merely know how to
find our way around in them for practical purposes.[62]

Eliot's discussion of "real" and "unreal" in these two
chapters seems to me to skirt a mystery, the mystery of
what is meant in Bradley by "my body." This is the same
mystery as how Shelley's white radiance ever gets frag-
mented by glass, or in Bradleian terms, how the Absolute
is pluralized in finite centers. Bradley frankly admits this
to be a problem beyond the scope of his metaphysics. I
would suspect—from the handling of the problem years

later in *Burnt Norton*—that Eliot skirts the whole subject because any explication of it would be mythic or
theological.[63] But when we have reached the point of asking what does the word "my" mean in *my body*, we are
ready for Eliot's discussion of the problem of solipsism
which he takes up in Chapter VI.

To illustrate the problem of the chapter, (again Eliot
is not responsible for the following illustration) imagine
the spectacle of a prize fight where 30,000 conscious spec-
tators watch two agents reduce one another to unconsciousness. If we keep to the abstract viewpoint of an
uninvolved philosopher, there would seem to be 30,002
windows in the white radiance ceaselessly focusing and re-
focusing images of the fight.

But what does it mean to say that the 30,002 windows
are screening the same fight? Does it mean that there is
one real fight and 30,002 impressions of it? No. There
are merely 30,002 impressions. There is no master photographic negative of which these are the 30,002 prints.[64]
But if this is so, has not Eliot's dissolution of Russell's
"real world out there" dissolved the possibility of *the*
fight and landed him squarely in the midst of the so-
called solipsistic dilemma? [65]

Eliot thinks not. The solipsistic dilemma, he believes,
is born of the confusion of two points of view. If we
look at the fight as we normally do from the standpoint
of what appears at one window, then there is one fight.
(Point of View A.) But if we contemplate the fight from
the standpoint of what appears in every window (something that we cannot do in actual practice, but do do theoretically as amateur philosophers asking questions) then
there are many fights. (Point of View B.) The solipsistic
dilemma is created when we take a stand with the philosopher and stand outside of any actual experience, and
yet also at the same time take a seat with the 30,000 spec-
tators and proceed to witness the fight with all of them.
Running back and forth between my own experience and
my neighbors', I naturally become aware only of the barriers that enclose one finite center from another.

The solipsistic dilemma is created when without actually taking any point of view we oscillate between many and so focus only the barriers that shut off one finite center from another. There is another way to synthesize these two necessary but seemingly contradictory points of view. Thus when I am actually watching the fight, I make the fight objective by taking account of other perspectives, my own as well as those of other persons. What gives my impression of the fight unity is the comparison and contrast, the allowance for interpretations, the idea-izing of my experience in the same way that I idea-ize the green blur on the highway as forest.[66] I make my impression fit a world. The reason I can do this is that the various points of view, my own and other persons, are all windows on *one* dome of glass opening on the one reality which is the white radiance. The only way the unity of reality can be realized is to pluralize it in the same way (the following illustration is Eliot's) that the only way I can be hit over the head with the *same* club is to be struck at least twice.[67] Just as the interweaving of perspectives produces the objective club, so the interweaving of 30,002 perspectives produces the objective fight.

The solipsistic dilemma turns out to be no dilemma at all. Though all our experiences are private, all of our ideas are common. To show that solipsism is true, someone would have to show that the content of one window is the content of one window and one window only.

Of interest in this chapter is the appearance for the first time in the dissertation of the terms "self" and "soul." Hitherto in the dissertation when Eliot had occasion to refer to us as subjects—that is to say as minds or states of consciousness—he had tended to dismiss us (very much as he dismisses the poet as personality in "Tradition and the Individual Talent"). "I" am a state of my objects, he declares early in the dissertation.[68] Consciousness, he says, may be reduced to relations between objects. "Mind," he will declare at the conclusion of the dissertation, is not a principle of explanation.[69]

But in the discussion of solipsism, of that point in his

scheme of things where the real and ideal intersect, a functional definition of "self" occurs. Suppose I look at a landscape from a church steeple, then from an airplane, then from a mountain top. Here are three points of view that have something in common. We cannot say that these three points of view are three aspects of "my" point of view, because as soon as a point of view is recognized it is transcended. Meanwhile we have got to have some identity of which to predicate the three viewpoints. The self is that identity.[70] Eliot says that this "self" is an ideal construction just as a world is.[71] At any given moment of vision, the self is no more present to awareness than is awareness of intercellular action.[72] But to say this is not to dismiss it as unimportant.

I am not sure that I know what Eliot is talking about in this regard. But perhaps a diagram will put us in a position where after a suitable interval understanding will follow. For some reason or other I find it difficult to think what Eliot means by "world" except by resorting to spatial analogies. Thus on the dome of glass, a world is a zone where objects of all one type exist together. Now the spatial analogy is misleading because we cannot say that the order exemplified as the biological world or the chemical world or the physical world is in space. Yet each world orders things and we think of things as stationary in space. (We ought not to, I know.) On the other hand, when I think of a string of moments of attention—which is about what a series of points of view is—I am driven to think in temporal terms. If I think of the self as a string of points on the dome of glass lighting up one after another in such a way as to make a streak of light, that streak might seem to typify the self. It is the residual unity seeming to hold together separate moments of consciousness.

The diagram is not very satisfactory. But it has one merit. It suggests that self and world are correlative terms. Thus a sea anemone eats his way toward a sea anemone's world (or toward consciousness of such a world), then constructs a sea anemone self to go with his world. Or this is what I infer Eliot is saying when he states that an ordinary person discovers his body and then constructs a self to go with it; [73] this is the self correlative with a physical world. But that such a self should exhaust a person's appetite for selfhood seems as unlikely as that conformity with my neighbor's image of me should afford me ultimate satisfactions. Eliot does not say this, but I think that we may safely say that once the white radiance appears in a finite center, that appearance is analogous to what in theological terms would be called an Incarnation. Thus "self" is an ideal which cannot rest anywhere short of the ultimate. It is the streak of light on the dome of glass that aims by circling to encompass the total white radiance.

But Eliot does not talk in these terms nor in these tones. What he says is that when B-point of view takes account of A-point of view, we are already at C-point of view, and that C-point of view by that point is no longer a center of feeling (a point of view) but a "self." [74] We do not properly say that B-point of view takes account of A-point of view, but that a "self" passes from A-point of view to B-point of view. "Point of view" is the crucial term in this discussion. In Eliot's usage, the term means "finite center." And in Bradley, finite center means one whole of feeling while it lasts.

If we ask, as Eliot does, what in one finite center is common property of several finite centers intending the same object, we are back at the prize fight at an Olympian point of view asking what the 30,002 windows have in common. Eliot's answer is interesting. They have, he says, nothing "really" in common, and everything ideally. [75] (The white radiance comes privately in other words to each window, but each window frame is part of one immense dome.) Eliot goes on to say that the reflection of reality in finite centers is not pluralism, because the centers are not things. [76] They are not "isolated." When we think of them as isolated we are not thinking of finite centers but of "souls"—i.e., our idea of something that "has" our experiences. We have now three distinctions:

(1) point of view (finite center, a moment of immediate experience); (2) soul (that finite center pictured as though it were a cell containing certain experiences); (3) self (a finite center pictured as linking together a sequence of centers).

But to come back to the problem of the chapter, Eliot's final word is that the solipsist would have to show that my "self" and its states were immediately given and other selves merely inferred.[77] But this is not the case. My self is as much an ideal construction as my construction of other people's persons. What is immediately given is a world, not a self, and the solipsist's question is therefore without meaning.

The conclusion of Eliot's dissertation has the atmosphere of a position won; it is full of final statements. For example, he characterizes the outlook he has come to as one which will forbid either an idealistic or a realistic philosophy at full value, though he believes that his final point of view will be found to be in agreement with Bradley's *Appearance and Reality*.[78] From absolute idealism he retains the notion of degrees of reality and that of the internality of relations. His idealism is objective: "consciousness," "activity of the mind" are rejected as principles of explanation. All objects are nonmental. The mental under investigation becomes mechanism; the physical becomes a mental construct. To inspect living mind we must examine the outer world.[79]

But when we ask what is the Conclusion about, we are at first hard pressed to say. Chapter I, we have said is about "experience"; Chapter II is about "thought." Chapters III, IV, and V are about "things," and Chapter VI is about "selves." What is there left to discuss? Our answer is found in the final word of the title: Knowledge.

The most interesting part of this discussion occurs when Eliot draws a distinction between knowledge and practical knowledge. Knowledge as such he suggests is not a relation between knower and known. It is merely one part of a spectacle, that context of ideality, I take it, that frames an object and makes it what it is for us.[80] But for the most part, knowledge is confused with practical knowledge. The latter, he says, is the narrowing of the context of an object to its relations to our bodies. It is this type of relationship that makes us think knowledge is the relation of knower to known. Eliot grants that knowledge of the physical world is the only demonstrable knowledge that we possess. He also grants that demonstrable truths are the only truths entitled to be called true. He declares himself to be as good a materialist as anybody.[81] But he here points out how short a way truths truly true carry us, and brings the discussion back to knowledge as distinct from practical knowledge, knowledge as it engages the attention of the metaphysician, the historian, and the literary critic.[82]

The truths that these men are engaged with are the truths, I take it, which have some sort of revelatory value. At the beginning of the dissertation, Eliot identified the real with immediate experience, that felt background out of which objects come and to which they return. Here we find him returning to that background. Our sense of the real is, he says, the criterion against which we project all of our theories. It is one and the same for all of us, until we try to describe it.[83]

There are several ways to rephrase what Eliot seems to be saying. One is his own formula: Metaphysics is inquiry into the point of view.[84] Translated this means: Metaphysics is knowledge of immediate experience. Still another is Eliot's statement that metaphysics is the effort to bend all points of view to one point of view.[85] Might we not translate this as the effort to bring all experiences into the unity of immediate experience?

But however phrased or paraphrased, what is interesting is the way Eliot lumps together at the end the metaphysician and the literary critic. Both must be, he says, scrupulous avoiders of formulae, refraining from statements that pretend to be literally true, aiming for truths of experience rather than truths of calculation.[86] Things collectively entertained, he says, are certainly not true; all significant truths are private truths. As they become public, they become facts, part of the public character, at worst catch-words.[87]

In short, the denial and the affirmation that Eliot ends with he expressed years later in *East Coker:*

> *There is, it seems to us,*
> *At best, only a limited value*
> *In the knowledge derived from experience.*
> *The knowledge imposes a pattern, and falsifies,*
> *For the pattern is new in every moment*
> *And every moment is a new and shocking*
> *Valuation of all we have been.*

And:

Home is where one starts from. As we grow older
The world becomes stranger, the pattern more complicated
Of dead and living. Not the intense moment
Isolated, with no before and after,
But a lifetime burning in every moment
And not the lifetime of one man only
But of old stones that cannot be deciphered.[88]

3   THE CRITICISM:
1917–1923

"Sound criticism is the application of a sound philosophy to works of art."—Stephen C. Pepper, The Basis of Criticism in the Arts.

In 1929, in an essay titled "Experiment in Criticism," T. S. Eliot declared that there is an urgent need for a criticism of a new kind that "will consist largely of a logical and dialectical study of the terms used." In the essay that follows, an attempt is made to make such an experiment. There have, of course, been many other such attempts since Eliot made his statement. If this one differs from others of its type, it does in the effort that is made to approach Eliot from a clearly defined standpoint, that of the metaphysics of his dissertation.

To do justice to Eliot's early criticism is hard work because of the number of considerations that have to be kept in mind simultaneously. We have, first, to think of that early criticism in the context of all of Eliot's work, prose and poetry. We have, second, to see it intervening between his doctoral dissertation (1916) and *The Waste Land* (1922). We have, third, to read all of it, or just about all of it, for some is not easy to obtain. We receive a different impression from such essays as "Tradition and the Individual Talent," "Hamlet," and "The Metaphysical Poets" when we see them in sequence with a hundred or so other articles that Eliot wrote between January, 1916, and November, 1923. Moreover, in speaking about

Eliot's work, as in thinking about any literary criticism, we have to spell out his critical presuppositions in advance and avoid, when exasperated, interpreting his utterances in a frame that is pseudoclassical (literature is the presentation of sound ideas in an attractive emotional context) or pseudoromantic (poetry is the overflow of emotion in a noninhibiting intellectual context). In addition, since literary criticism is probably like theology in that the basic statements are figurative, we have to avoid taking Eliot literally. His criticism is not about literary "things," for a poem is not a thing the way a carrot is a carrot; criticism is about *acts* fundamentally mysterious since they are not acts in the ordinary sense. They are not transformations of an environment by one physical body operating on other physical bodies, but transfigurations of a situation by a self's transformation of itself. Still further, in considering what Eliot says we have frequently to suspend judgment on the rightness or wrongness of his individual judgments, or their specific importance or unimportance, in order to concentrate on the concept of the literary act that his ideas are pointing at. His practical criticism is, perhaps, theoretical criticism, an instrument, mainly, for elucidating literary principles. Finally, we have to know something of the epistemological system, the terms of which control the terms of Eliot's literary criticism; we have, in short, to be sensitive to the philosophical nuances of words like "object," "feeling," "ideas," "point of view" as Eliot uses them. It is somewhat surprising that many expositors of Eliot who would not think of interpreting what Aristotle means by "mimesis" apart from his other writings and apart from his frame of reference, or what Coleridge means by "imagination" apart from his total effort as poet and theorist, have ventured to show what Eliot means by "tradition," "objective correlative," "dissociation of sensibility" without putting those terms into a fairly complicated context. But Eliot, of course, has been a somewhat indifferent parent to his critical ideas, leaving them like infants on various doorsteps, allowing other people to raise them, and acknowledging only those whose faces make up well.

In the experiment that follows so much effort goes into setting up lights and fixing focusing devices, the elements to be focused sometimes seem to be hemmed in by a forest of fixtures. There seemed no way to avoid this, and this introductory statement is an attempt to say why.

ii

If Eliot's beginning as a poet is a metaphysical standpoint, it is tempting to see his early, and most influential criticism as the application of a philosophy to literature. Because it is fragmentary although voluminous, it is exasperating; and yet because it is the response of a young poet schooled in philosophy to a problem at once personal and cultural, it is significant and emotionally charged to a degree unusual in criticism. To ask what this criticism means is to ask two questions. What did the poet write it for? and what "idea" explains and reconciles puzzling and seemingly discrepant utterances?

The answers here proposed (but proposed more as useful hypotheses than as theses literally true) are that Eliot wrote his early criticism to keep himself persuaded that poetry could be written in an unpoetic age by a poet from whom the muse had departed, and to persuade others that though the poetry business was, indeed, in a bankrupt state, it was so because of the misapplication of reason and could be restored by reviving an old line of goods—"intellectual," or philosophic poetry—which, however difficult, and dry, and prosaic, not only was intensely poetic but was the one right poetry for an age of unbelief.

In declining to offer these answers as literally true, I am trying to avoid the suggestion that these hypotheses reveal what Eliot consciously and literally was moved by in the years 1917–23. On different occasions, Eliot himself has testified to different motives for his criticism—that he was moved by the need to make small sums of money quickly; [1] that he was moved by a concern that the integrity of poetry be respected, i.e. that poetry be judged as poetry and not another thing; [2] and that he was moved by the need to make a place for the kind of poetry he wanted himself to write. [3]

The idea that Eliot's early criticism is exciting because it has an emotional charge on it, and that this charge is due to the fact that he is responding to a personal as well as a cultural predicament is a supposition on my part. But certain facts seem to support it. Eliot does seem to have been one whom (as he said of Donne and Coleridge [4]) the muse visited early and then abandoned, leaving him a person who might have made something of his life, but for the muse. His philosophical studies do appear to have coincided with a period of poetic nonactivity [5] and may have been undertaken to redeem the time, to assist a man who had been a poet at twenty-one to be a poet after twenty-five. [6] His early critical activities, moreover, do coincide with a period of pump-priming; when incapable of versifying in English, he began to compose in French, with fruitful results. [7] One might guess, therefore, that though Eliot may have written to convert others, he wrote also to cheer himself up, to preserve the conviction that it was possible to construct something poetic on which to rejoice.

Starting, however, from the supposition that there is a central motive in Eliot's early criticism, and the assumption that there is a controlling idea, I must inevitably see more pattern in Eliot's random critical utterances than the poet himself perhaps saw (I doubt this) or professes to see now, and certainly more than many of his critics have observed. As is well known, the critical Eliot has been charged with contradicting himself on every important issue he took up, betraying inherent incapacity for theoretical thought, and playing Dr. Jekyll in the criticism and Mr. Hyde in the poetry. [8] Anyone who has tried to read straight through the *Selected Essays* will sympathize with these adverse criticisms. If, as Eliot declared in his dissertation, the aim of the critic should be to avoid public formulae, [9] he succeeded in his aim beyond expectation. But what Eliot once remarked about Pascal's *Pensées* is probably the truth about his criticism: "He who reads this . . . will observe at once its fragmentary nature, but only after some study will perceive the fragmentariness lies in the expression more than in the thought." [10]

The problem that is a context for Eliot's criticism is, by now, an old one. A personal expression of it was Coleridge's lament for the loss of his "shaping power of imagination" in Stanza VI of "Dejection: an Ode," which Eliot once said constituted for him "one of the saddest confessions that I have ever read." [11] An equally personal, semiphilosophic, semiliterary expression of the problem was Nietzsche's *The Birth of Tragedy*, whole passages of which echo in Eliot's *The Waste Land*. Nietzsche's formulation was: "Yet every culture that has lost myth has lost, by the same token, its natural healthy creativity. Only a horizon ringed about with myths can unify a culture. . . . Man today, stripped of myth, stands famished among all his pasts and must dig frantically for roots, be it among the most remote antiquities." [12] I. A. Richards' *Science and Poetry* (1926) is a contemporary analysis of the problem, one that Eliot said awakened him to the fact that there is a problem of different types of belief, one that he criticized for its naturalistic theory of value, and one that he praised for anticipating the question that the next generation will be putting to themselves. [13]

But the problem—how to be a poet in a world from which the element of depth has vanished—though easy to feel, is less easy to formulate in neutral language. Here (to keep connections with previous chapters), I shall think of it as the problem created by the decay of valid metaphysical sensibility. To follow Eliot's dealings with the question, I shall attempt to provide two formulas— one for the concept of the poetic act that seems to underlie Eliot's early criticism and one for the four dimensions of that act that we need to take account of if we are to follow Eliot's diagnostic treatment of the literary ailments of his own and earlier ages. Only after these are out of the way can we come to the real point of the essay— Eliot's prescription of a kind of poetry appropriate to an "Alexandrian" culture.

iii

Although Eliot in the thirties denied having a general theory of literature to offer, [14] his early criticism implies a poetics—an idea of what poetry is and does.[15] There are many partial observations in Eliot's early criticism of how poets work, but these usually terminate just at the point where a philosophic point of view is involved.[16] It is as though Eliot either knew his over-all position so well that he had no need to place literature in a total framework, or that he was sensitive to the difficulty of talking metaphysics in a poetry session. (Coleridge erred frequently in this regard.) But anyone who wants to think through Eliot's criticism must see it in conjunction with a philosophy. Here the difficulties arise that force me to supply two formulas seemingly out of thin air.

Eliot's practical criticism implies a poetics, but that poetics is hard to describe in complete terms because somewhere between Eliot's dissertation (which is a fact) and Eliot's criticism (which is a fact), a third linking fact is missing. We could say that what is missing in an anthropology, a theory of man. Eliot's dissertation is a theory of knowing without a knower, just as his criticism is a theory of writing without a writer. I am using "anthropology" in a sense so broad that, taking it in terms of the kind of metaphysics Eliot worked out in his thesis, his statement of an anthropology would actually turn out to be a theology—a statement of man's involvement in, estrangement from, and soteriological relation to an Absolute. Much later, it will be recalled, Eliot declared that no literary criticism can be substantive except in the framework of a theology [17]—but we have no such documentary evidence of it as we have of Eliot's epistemology. All we know is that in a seminar of Josiah Royce's in 1913 he was studying the relation between description and interpretation, and reading widely in anthropology, and asserting on at least one occasion that truths imply contexts of belief.[18] It is possible to detect certain theological leanings in some of Eliot's philosophic book reviews (1916–19) for the *International Journal of Ethics*.[19] But no one has ever investigated this matter, and it would be hazardous to try to do so here.

We could say (and it adds up ultimately to the same

thing [20]) that the missing element is a theory of language which the dissertation points to but does not supply and the criticism takes for granted but does not provide. Throughout the dissertation significant declarations about language are thrown out by the way as it were, but the involvement of linguistic and knowing processes is never directly taken up. For example, Eliot remarks that we make a mistake to think of language as merely a development of our ideas; it is a development of reality as well.[21] Taken in one light, this observation may seem tame: Eliot is merely saying that language develops what is felt as well as what is thought. But taken in another light, Eliot's innocuous observation is saying that we are what we say and giving a new reality to the Biblical statement that no word shall be lost, and every word uttered shall be judged.[22] We see, on another level, why Eliot in his dissertation dwells on the peculiar anachronism of a contemporary geologist describing an earlier world in a language subsequently developed.[23] Thus, Eliot's entire dissertation might be interpreted as a discourse on language, language regarded not as a set of things called words, but a set of acts whereby an organism which is part of the universe becomes sufficiently social to contemplate that universe of which it is an organ. When, in *The Sacred Wood* Eliot says that "permanent literature" is always a "presentation," either a "presentation of thought," as in Aristotle, who strips thought to its essential structure, or a "presentation of feeling by a statement of events in human action or objects in the external world,"[24] as in the *Agamemnon* or *Macbeth*, revealing "the essential sickness or strength of the human soul,"[25] he is making a basic statement about the two rhythms that govern language. By one the organism fixes a world (glimpses the mysterious order of the concepts); by another it takes possession of a self—sees who the person is who has been constituted by his choices.

What is striking about Eliot's description of the second type of permanent literature is that it leaves an impression (encouraged elsewhere) that Eliot's poetics is basically Aristotelian.[26] Poetry for him is an "imitation of an action." But Aristotle's famous formula, having been affixed to Eliot, needs to be clarified. Could we say that poetry is an imitation of an action (men feeling and doing something) in order to create an imitation Action (man recognizing and affirming his destiny by re-enactment), we would be approaching the concept of literature that lurks behind Eliot's early criticism. But to clarify the difference between action (a corporeal matter) and Action (a linguistic), I must step outside Eliot's criticism and resort to a formula taken from R. G. Collingwood's *Principles of Art*. Collingwood's concept of art-as-language (which Eliot evidently read with interest in the 1940's [27]) seems very close to what Eliot might have come up with had he been forced to propound a theory of art on an examination in 1916.

Imagine a baby lying contentedly and silently in his crib. Suddenly an elder child steals up and drops a red silk handkerchief over the baby's eyes and blinds his vision. The baby cries aloud. The baby's cry illustrates what Collingwood calls an expression, but not language. Consider a second illustration.

I walk toward a porch where my fiancée is when her Airedale leaps from his hiding place and snaps and snarls at me. I jump. Collingwood would put my jump in the same category as the baby's cry: psychic expression, but not language.[28]

Suppose, now, that I walk toward the porch and the dog still advances with me, snapping and snarling. Being afraid of dogs, I cannot avoid flinching at every other step, ignominious behaviour that I focus from my fiancée's point of view. How can she possibly love me? At a stroke, the dog has deprived me of self and world and reduced me to a thing at the mercy of brute things.

Suppose, however, that while behaving no differently, I manage to consider the whole situation as a spectacle: dog, personal terror, humiliating responses. I should be bringing what Collingwood calls consciousness into play, and transforming the original sensations and emotions into what Collingwood calls imagination, a more or less stable mosaic of raw experience frozen for contempla-tion.[29]

Collingwood emphasizes that consciousness has a liber-ating effect on me. Sensation and emotion cease to be something imposed from without and tend to become something *I* have, even though having them is not one of my prized possessions. But as yet I do not have language. I have psychic expression (my cringe before the dog) and imagination (my picture of the total situation).

But, now, suppose that with an imaginative eye on my fiancée, on myself, and on the dog, I recollect a dance where my fiancée broke the heel of her dancing slipper. I recall her expression of reproach as she looked at the heel, apology as she glanced at me, and then I remember her shrug as she resumed the dance. Suppose now that I imitate her behaviour and do it in such a way that I see that she recognizes what I am doing. If I understand Col-lingwood, I am still flinching in front of the dog, but I am flinching and shrugging at the same time. My composite action becomes a kind of dance.[30] My psychic expression has become imaginative expression or language, low-level language it is true, nevertheless language and art. The complex act, not only catches up all the pieces of the sit-uation held by my imagination, it not only duplicates the psychic cringe, it also expresses my sense of liberation, my emotion of delight at being able to transfigure my involun-tary behaviour. Thus the emotion expressed is unique. My act expresses both my involvement in the world of neces-sity and my freedom from it.

Collingwood's "language," it should be clear, is not what most people think of when they think of "lan-guage." That word ordinarily calls to mind what Colling-wood calls an "intellectual symbolism."[31] He insists, how-ever, that we shall never comprehend the real nature of language if we start to think about it at the level of intel-lectual symbolism, or scientific discourse. Scientific dis-course is the top level of a mode of behaviour that is more analogous to dance than to discourse. And scientific dis-course withers and dies unless it retains its roots in imaginative expression, which in turn is rooted in psychic expression. In an early essay, when Eliot declares that "all thought and all language is based ultimately on a few simple physical movements" [32] he is expressing a point of view similar to Collingwood's as well as one consistent with the epistemological views expressed in the dissertation. The objects that confront us are what they are first because of the kind of physical organisms we are.

But what might be of use here is the way Collingwood's art-as-imaginative-expression combines two old positions in literary criticism and perhaps permits us to interpret Eliot's Aristotelian poetics in a post-Crocean way. In literary criticism there have been not too many basic perspectives that produce fruitful results in practical criticism. From the classic period we inherit the Aristotelian viewpoint (poetry is an imitation) [33] and the Longinian (sublimity is the echo of a great soul).[34] Both these approaches were one-sided. Aristotle's focus showed so clearly what art comes from that what it moves toward came out blurred. To unimaginative successors Aristotle's insight became a public formula that art mirrors life for pleasure or instruction. The distinctiveness of the end of art was lost. That Aristotle meant more seems certainly possible. Mimesis, interpreted in the light of his characteristic philosophic tendencies, ought to have meant a two-way process, taking life as it appears in a flesh and blood context and putting that appearance into a context of art so that something only potential in the flesh and blood world becomes actual in the world of art. What the something is that is actualized in the mimetic context (and only in the mimetic context) Aristotle either could not clarify or did not feel the need to clarify; he called it "catharsis," a term that has puzzled his commentators.

Longinus, on the other hand, judging that writers gained an immortality of fame from sublimity—a certain excellence of style that echoes a great soul and evokes transport in the reader—focused so sharply what art moves toward that what it moves from was left blurry. We are uncertain what differentiates the echo of a great soul from the roar of an African lion.

A double-barreled formula like Collingwood's has the best of both points of view. A poem is both mimetic (i.e. imaginative) and expressive. When I find a way voluntarily to re-enact my involuntary response to a dog, I have acted both mimetically and expressively; I have imitated my psychic expression but imitated it in such circumstances that my imitation is an expression of the emotion of transcending my initial emotion. I have thus exemplified "catharsis," Aristotelian catharsis interpreted, not as extrinsic to the art act, but inherent in it, being that liberation from brute environment that language affords. At the same time, I have illustrated "sublimity"—a way of "speaking" that fills the soul with joy and vaunting, a transport that no lion's roar can sound because it comes from one's recognition of being a self in a human community.

But the crucial feature in the development of imaginative expression, i.e. language, is something that Collingwood's formula takes for granted and does not emphasize to any great extent. We need to emphasize it because of the fundamental importance to understanding the problem, at once personal and cultural, that Eliot faced as a literary critic. This is the factor of a community of interpretation, the kind of community that, at the lowest level, exists between me and my fiancée because of common feelings and memories. This community of interpretation manifests itself in two quite different ways. It operates first to provide me with that impersonal perspective that deprives me of my assumed self. (I see myself, that is, from my girl's point of view as a shameful coward.) It operates, second, to provide me with a remembered gesture that enables me to restore my self. (I see my shameful behaviour as a reenactment of my fiancée's behaviour, so that not I but "we" respond to the dog.)

These two modes of focusing a situation correspond to Eliot's two forms of permanent literature. Both, it seems apparent, are rooted in one community of interpretation. I cannot see the facts of my behaviour except *from* my fiancée's point of view; I cannot re-enact those facts except *to* her point of view, which incidentally is not *hers,* but *ours*. Nevertheless, though rooted in one community of interpretation, the first perspective, defining what Josiah Royce called the world of description, tends to cut me off from my roots, to destroy what Royce called the world of appreciation.[35] What would happen if through some hypertrophy of the first organ of seeing, we all focused the world of description so compellingly that we lost the capacity to see the community between persons that every act of language implies and thus lost the capacity to believe in any real community between persons? Such a hypothetical situation is exemplified in "The Love Song of J. Alfred Prufrock" where the "eyes that fix you in a formulated phrase" have made the community between persons unsee-able. Moreover, our hypothetical situation is one more or less equivalent to that precipitated for us by the massive successes in the seventeenth, eighteenth, and nineteenth centuries of the scientific way of seeing. Here, with what I. A. Richards called the "neutralization of nature" [36]—a phrase which means the loss of a sense of community of interpretation—is the problem with which Eliot's criticism begins.

iv

Eliot's problem as poet-critic may now be formulated several ways, all of which eventually add up to the same thing. We could say that the problem was metaphysical: the loss of a community of interpretation was due to the decay of metaphysical sensibility. Or we could say that the problem was literary. The decay of metaphysical sensibility was due to the weakening of a valid poetic tradition. Or we could say that the problem was educational. The abandonment of the poetic tradition was due to the rise of science. Or we could say that the problem was cultural: the rise of an urban industrialized world created an environment that seemed to deny human community.

But if we are to talk about Eliot's literary criticism, we need to restrict attention to the language act, and yet to stratify our initial general impression of that act so as to see its four-sided character. For the sake of easy remembering, then, and to keep the different dimensions of Eliot's diagnostics clear, I am going to suggest that the language act—taking it from the poet's point of view—be thought of as like Aristotle's cosmic process, involving four "causes." There is the material cause, which, in Aristotle's terms, is something to be moved, and which, in my illustration would seem to be my fiancée's Airedale, and the whole realm of physical necessity that he implies. There is the efficient cause, something in Aristotle's terms, to do the moving, and in my illustration is the point of view of my observant fiancée. There is the formal cause, which, in Aristotle, is the path toward the goal, and which, in my illustration, is the remembered dance. There is the final cause, which, in Aristotle, is the point where the process comes to rest, and which, in my illustration, would be the restored community involving me, my fiancée, and the Airedale. Let me illustrate what the poetic process looks like when viewed in terms of four "causes," using wherever possible references drawn from Eliot's early criticism, but supplementing these with whatever others seem useful.

We must begin with the final cause. In the case of my danced cringe, the final cause, what I am aiming for, is the sense of fulfillment that comes when I have fused into one significant whole the Airedale, the dread, the humiliation and the community between myself and fiancée. In "Tradition and the Individual Talent" (where Eliot warns that it is not the sublimity of the felt materials that makes art great, but the intensity of the process whereby they fuse) Eliot speaks of halting at the frontier of metaphysics. No theory of literature resembling Eliot's can really do so. Thus in *The Dry Salvages* when Eliot speaks of hearing music so deeply that you are the music while the music lasts, he names this experience an "Incarnation." [37] This, of course, is a late work (1941). Nevertheless, in an early piece of criticism, we find Eliot acknowledging the metaphysical dimension of the final cause of the art process: "The end of the enjoyment of poetry is a pure contemplation from which all the accidents of personal emotion are removed; thus we aim to see the object as it really is and find a meaning for the words of Arnold. And without a labour which is largely a labour of the intelligence, we are unable to attain that stage of vision *amor intellectualis Dei.*" [38]

Elsewhere when he speaks of fusion and unity of feeling,[39] he is back in the context of the poetic act, and using words that are misleading unless they are re-related to the miraculous. What is fused is not merely this superficial feeling with that, but the whole being of the poet and the reader with a situation. What makes the experience ecstatic is that it offers release from our sense of separateness. Since there are no novelties in literary criticism or philosophy, there is nothing original in Eliot's notion of the end of the poetic process. His *fusion* seems another name for that reconciliation of opposites that Coleridge speaks of as the ultimate goal of poetic imagination.[40]

But the final cause is not a term to be comprehended apart from the material cause. In *The Cocktail Party*, Harcourt-Reilly describes the experience of being suddenly reduced to the status of an object:

> *When you've dressed for a party*
> *And are going downstairs, with everything about you*
> *Arranged to support you in the role you have chosen,*
> *Then sometimes, when you come to the bottom step*
> *There is one step more than your feet expected*
> *And you come down with a jolt. Just for a moment*
> *You have the experience of being an object*
> *At the mercy of a malevolent staircase.*[41]

Here we have an evocation of what I mean by the material cause of a poem. What is it? It is any situation, any organization of experience that reduces a person to a thing. When my fiancée's Airedale deprives me of my self and my world, he has introduced me to the material cause of a poem. Of course, poems do not necessarily start from the material cause. They may start with transport (the final cause), or with a conventional form, or an idea, as well as with a depersonalized situation. But wherever in actual practice the poem starts, the material cause will be the Caliban who is Ariel's opposite. Eliot in his early criticism does not phrase the matter just this way. He merely emphasizes that art starts with the physiological, an actual brain in an actual environment, our "personal animal feelings," "our exact and practical passions." [42] Then he goes on to speak of the poet as seeking to transmute our practical responses to our physical environment. He stresses that what makes a poet a poet is his inability to trim his feelings to fit the "quotidian." The poet is compelled to "extend" (another recurrent Eliot term) [43] his feelings until he finds a point from which the quotidian is transformed in a new whole. The shock of surprise that Eliot finds great poetry provides [44] comes, I infer, from our finding the world of flesh and blood completely transfigured while remaining flesh and blood. The poet regains his personality by becoming a new person. He does so by transforming the material cause into "matter" for art.

The efficient cause in the poetic process (something to do the moving) is simply good sense, or what the Augustans would have called good sense. Eliot sometimes calls it "wit." [45] If genius is required to see the obvious, Eliot's critical genius is best illustrated by his clear view of the role of intelligence in the poetic process. Indebted as he is to Matthew Arnold's perception that the main fault in romantic art is not lack of poetic genius but lack of wit,[46] Eliot goes beyond Arnold by virtue of his having a theory of language. Eliot sees that the role of knowledge in art is not to furnish the artist material, but to enable him to define exactly what and how much he feels in a given situation.

Harcourt-Reilly (*The Cocktail Party*) again furnishes us an elementary lesson in poetics.[47] He shows how wit works in a poetic progression. Edward Chamberlayne has been reduced to the status of an object by virtue of the departure of his wife on the eve of a cocktail party. What does Reilly do? He calls for gin and water and gives Edward a clairvoyant description, from a devil's point of view, of the profit and loss of a wifeless situation. What is the effect? Edward sees what he really does feel in the situation, and becomes dimly conscious of how much his feeling exceeds what he would feel were he merely an object in a world of malevolent objects. I call "wit" the efficient cause because it is the first step whereby the poet *moves* that organization of experience he is against.

Eliot's discussions of what I call the efficient cause in the poetic process do not necessarily recognize a difference between the efficient and formal dimensions of the process. It is profitable for us, nevertheless, to observe a distinction between the kind of attention that defines the material cause and the kind of attention which finds a way to the final cause. What I mean by the efficient cause is most clearly placed by Eliot in early essays [48] when he observes that it is only by the exercise of intelligence that we avoid "rhetoric;" intelligence enables us to determine exactly what and how much we feel in a given situation. "Intelligence" as Eliot uses the term is a characteristic of educated consciousness.[49] It is the ability to see from a social perspective what Josiah Royce calls "the world of description." In the essay on Marvell, Eliot calls this "wit," and speaks of it as an ability to see an experience from the point of view of other experiences. It is a quality he finds lacking in artists like Blake and D. H. Lawrence.[50]

The formal cause in the poetic process is the hardest to talk about. It is not identifiable with external forms like blank verse, sonnet form, the five act plot, or even quantity of sounds of English words, or figuration.[51] Although without these the formal cause cannot exist, it itself, like Henry James' "figure in the carpet" escapes public formulation. When the poet is in motion, it is the pattern that Eliot speaks of in *Burnt Norton* whereby the poem reaches the stillness; at the moment of flight, it is not merely certain conventions, but the readiness of a public to respond to these—what Eliot in another place calls the "temper of an age." [52]

The earlier illustration of my fiancée's Airedale may make clear three characteristics of a formal cause: (1) it must involve a convention common to me and my fiancée; (2) it must have the power to reproduce in some fashion my psychic response to her dog; (3) it must "reach the stillness," i.e. restore the sense of community destroyed by the dog's attack. The recollected dance had these characteristics.

But this illustration serves notice, again, that what is crucial in the poetic process is a community of interpretation. Without that, art seems not possible. The kind of community required, moreover, is not furnished by such naturalistic activities as a beaux art ball, or the firemen's annual Fourth of July picnic—or is not insofar as these involve the extinction of the person in a collectivity. The kind of association involved, as Josiah Royce pointed out, is one where the individual finds himself realized in the group.[53]

The formal cause of a poem, then, is a social entity of the kind Josiah Royce has in mind when he speaks of a church, or Eliot when he speaks of a literary tradition. The essence of what Eliot has to say about the formal cause is contained in "Tradition and the Individual Talent." But Eliot's determination in that piece to avoid the metaphysical, makes his declarations somewhat cryptic.

If we take Eliot's essay, however, in conjunction with the characteristics of a formal cause already illustrated we see why Eliot stresses such points as the absolute difference between an event and an art event.[54] My response to a dog and my mimetic dance of that response are not in the same sphere of being. We see too why Eliot insists that the most original parts of a poet's work may be those points where the dead poets, his ancestors, make their presences felt. I must be invaded, as it were, by the ghost of my fiancée's behaviour before I can join together the fragments of the situation.[55] We understand, in addition, why Eliot judges many readers to be capable of the experience of sincere emotion in a poem (i.e. the sincerity of my response to the dog) and some readers to be capable of appreciating technical excellence (i.e. my skill in graceful mimicry), but very few to be able to see a significant emotion in a poem, an emotion having its life in the poem and not the history of the poet.

Eliot's last statement invites the interpretation that a poem does not express what a man in a situation feels, but what the man feels in that situation as a representative of a community. It is the sensibility of the community that speaks, just as in Nietzsche's interpretation of Greek tragedy, the sensibility of the audience is given back by the protagonist through the mediating vision of the chorus.[56]

But if, having glimpsed what in the poetic process the formal cause is, we now return to Eliot's problem as a poet-critic, we do so with the impression that his problem was insoluble. It is as though he were asking me to invent a dance to transmute my emotion in the presence of a fiancée that I know to be a fool—a fiancée, that is, who not only disapproves of dancing, but has been educated to believe that two and only two responses are appropriate to an unruly dog: (1) scientific lectures on care and training of dogs; (2) "poetic" falsifications of the unpleasant facts such that I am enabled to pretend no dog is there.

In "Tradition and the Individual Talent," Eliot is discussing, it would appear, only half of the formal problem —the relation of the poet to his dead ancestors. What of the poet's relation to his contemporaries? A tradition not exemplified in what George Herbert Mead called "the generalized other" is not alive. Was Eliot's problem not merely that of living in an age that was "formless" but one where counterfeit forms had driven out good? He formulated the matter in these terms in 1920 in "The Possibility of a Poetic Drama." After stating that "no man can invent a form, create a taste for it, and perfect it to," and pointing out how fortunate Shakespeare was to have "given into one's hands, a crude form, capable of indefinite refinement," he concluded, "But it is now very questionable whether there are more than two or three in the present generation who are *capable*, the least little bit, of benefiting by such advantages were they given." [57]

v

The path through Eliot's criticism is strewn with terminological mementoes of his struggle to solve the seemingly insoluble problem of how to write poetry in a formless age. His path is crooked and many of his terms do not systematize very neatly. But if we remember that Eliot was a poet with a metaphysic and a literary critic convinced that the real world *is* a community, then the problem seems less insoluble. Eliot's early criticism becomes an interesting three-phase therapeutic operation. In phase one, he surveys malformations occurring in the literary body when writers lose contact with a metaphysical center. "Dissociation of sensibility" is the memento of this phase of the operation. Milton, Dryden, Tennyson, and Swinburne are some of the patients. In phase two, he demonstrates some of the wrong measures intelligent poets took when confronted by loss of depth, either in themselves or in their society. "Objective correlative," "tradition" are the mementoes of this stage; Shakespeare and Blake are the subjects. In phase three, the physician prescribes a right way to write when the social atmosphere is dry. "Poetry of design" is the most memorable of his terms. Ben Jonson on the English side, Henry James on the American, are the examples.

Eliot's terminological mementoes are keys to the various phases of his literary-critical operation. None is more important than dissociation of sensibility,[58] and none harder to treat. To interpret it we need a concept and the one I start with derives from reading Eliot's criticism against his dissertation. Dissociation of sensibility is the dislocation of thought from feeling and feeling from thought that occurs when language orbits too far out from a metaphysical center (a metaphor borrowed from the beginning of *Choruses from "The Rock"*) and spurious centers are established, the center of the restrictedly objective, or of the restrictedly subjective. The cause of the dissociation is faulty metaphysical vision that leads either to the absolutizing of some specific view (some order) or some specific point of view (some means of visualizing an order) instead of *the* point of view which cannot be fixed in any view or specific point of view. Thus when the literary process sickens, declines, and finally breaks down, the source of the malady is some such error of philosophic judgment as Bertrand Russell (rightly or wrongly) is found guilty of in Chapter IV of Eliot's dissertation. The error is that of confusing a practical point of view with an ultimate one and substituting the physically real for the metaphysically real. But the error is inherent in the nature of language, and dissociation of sensibility would seem, therefore, to be an inevitable accompaniment of all maturation of language. The better a language is, the better we objectify a world; the better we objectify a world, the more easily we are taken captive by it. Perhaps one of Eliot's somewhat puzzling remarks on two early manifestations of dissociated sensibility may make plausible this concept of dissociation of sensibility. In "John Dryden" (1921) Eliot implies, I believe, that Milton and Dryden have equally "commonplace" minds.[59] "Commonplace," in the context, seems to mean metaphysically obtuse, and supports the interpretation that dissociation of sensibility is merely a literary-critical term for loss of metaphysical sensibility. Now the intent of Eliot's remark is clear. It is to startle us into an evaluation of Milton's vision, to force us to weigh the poet's tendency in *Paradise Lost*, to treat realistically matters that are not material and not susceptible of literal statement. But the point I aim to make is that such illustrations of high level, but "commonplace" minding as Milton and Dryden exemplify are symptoms of materialization of thought occurring simultaneously with a growth of scientific language and an increasing objectification of a physical world. Soon abstract universals become deified "things" as in the eighteenth-century popular philosophers' apotheosis of Newton's law of gravitation. Thereafter, the pendulum swings again and the deified world-machine is a Frankenstein monster (as Milton's God becomes a devil to Shelley), and romanticism, the heretical reaction to a heresy sets in. Aesthetic feeling divorced from reason is enthroned as an absolute in place of the discredited universal. The end of the course appears: a Browning fabricating a world out of private ideals, a Swinburne one out of private sensations, and a Tennyson, oscillating between, now anaesthetizing his feelings in

order to kneel before Victorian ideas so sanctified by public opinion that he dared not question them, and now
anaesthetizing his ideas in order to find relief for his feelings. Eliot's sympathetic analysis of Tennyson's predicament (in "In Memoriam") is a fine thing. But for the
diagnostician, the cause of the "dissociation of sensibility"
comes down finally to a writer's compulsion to provide an
illegitimate satisfaction for the metaphysical instinct of a
society that has lost its metaphysical eyes. Or so it seems
to me. The essay that comes closest to revealing the
syndrome is Eliot's "The Possibility of a Poetic Drama"
(1920) where the connection between literary formless-
ness and impure literary motivation is illustrated (rightly
or wrongly) by Goethe, the "philosophic poet," who doctors the facts of existence with ideas in order to fabricate
a world his heart can rest in, and by Bergson, the "poetic"
philosopher, who doctors the facts of life with feelings in
order to fabricate a world his head can find tolerable.
Here we sense that Eliot's "dissociated sensibility" is
closely akin to R. G. Collingwood's "corrupt consciousness."

No one, of course, can read Eliot's scattered remarks on
dissociation of sensibility without realizing that the term
points in half a dozen directions at once at phenomena
occurring on different planes of experience. Eliot used it
to classify pathological symptoms in the language process
with no intimations given that the term had a philosophical background. His readers not having enjoyed the benefit
of conversion by F. H. Bradley were unaware that the
"union in all perception of thought with sense, the co-
presence everywhere in all appearances of fact with ideality
—this is the one foundation of truth." [60] They were unaware that unified and dissociated sensibility are matters
of degree; no human mind is ever fully unified, none ever
fully dissociated. Nor were they warned that when a high
degree of dissociation occurs in a culture, literary men can
probably not do much about it on their own hook. A
metaphysical change of climate is occurring and a metaphysician is called for to chart where we are. But in phase

one of his operation, Eliot was perhaps less interested in theorizing than in classifying the classic symptoms that crop up at every level of the literary process when metaphysical awareness evaporates. He resembled a practitioner fresh from medical school filling his office with bottled specimens of the pathological. Here, illustrative of the onset of the dissociation is John Dryden: atrophy of the final cause.[61] Here, illustrative of the end is Charles Algernon Swinburne: atrophy of the material cause.[62] Here exemplifying symptoms at the middle of the way is William Blake: progressive deterioration of the formal cause.[63] Here nearing the end is Alfred Lord Tennyson: loss of the efficient cause.[64]

Eliot's exercises in literary pathology hardly helped him, however, to deal with the sickness of language as it affected him. What could the poet do to be well? In the second phase of the operation we see him showing what measures not to take. William Blake, in the prophetic books, and Shakespeare in *Hamlet* are the subjects. Two more terms, "tradition" and "objective correlative" are memorials of the moment.

William Blake's predicament was to be caught in a cultural context where the final cause of the literary act had sunk from sight, and his wrong move was to attempt to remedy the situation by becoming a one-man poet, prophet, and propagandist coercing a society into seeing with his metaphysical vision. He provides Eliot an instructive example of the point where a unified sensibility turns and becomes dissociated. He begins as a "naked man" whose work has the same terrifying honesty as that of Aeschylus, Dante, Villon, or Shakespeare. In his early work he presents vision, which means that, partly by virtue of his education, he is able to use ideas as idea-ings to define feeling instead of as sacred pillars of the eighteenth-century firmament. But the later Blake reverses the order and makes feeling the servant of ideas. His prophetic books betray, according to Eliot, a tendency to be formless. It is not that they are too visionary, but not visionary enough, Eliot states. We might judge that Blake had been taken captive by his own abstractions.

When Eliot concludes that what Blake's genius needed "was a framework of accepted and traditional ideas which would have prevented him from indulging in a philosophy of his own, and concentrated attention upon the problems of the poet," he is writing a prescription, not for Blake, but for himself. When he looks at Blake, he is intent on analyzing the response of a man of genius to an arid cultural situation: "The fault is perhaps not with Blake himself, but with the environment which failed to provide what such a poet needed; perhaps the circumstances compelled him to fabricate, perhaps the poet required the philosopher and mythologist; although the conscious Blake may have been quite unconscious of his motives." [65] Eliot might well have been cautioning himself.

Shakespeare's wrong movement in *Hamlet* might seem to illustrate the exact opposite of Blake's. Blake had so clear a vision of the end to be attained that he tried to drive his readers toward it without regard to their habitual reaction patterns. He violated the formal cause. Shakespeare was so sensible of the need to play the literary game according to the established rules that he allowed the public formulas of his profession to dominate his vision. He betrays the final cause. But the terms of Eliot's diagnostic (in "Hamlet and his Problems," 1919) when applied to Shakespeare's movements seemed calculated to produce a maximum of mystification. How, one wondered, if Lady Macbeth washing her hands is an "objective correlative" can Hamlet playing the buffoon before Ophelia avoid being one too? But the question shows that we are seeing the objective correlative as a material factor rather than a formal one in the artistic act. Blake's failure to be visionary enough in the prophetic books might be called a failure to find an objective correlative. For the term means the *way* to what has been termed the final cause. Shakespeare took a way to his vision that went in the opposite direction from his vision. His state of mind (and now I am putting together hints that Eliot drops in separate later essays) was peculiar; he was undergoing the condition of aridity that is one phase of the movement toward religious commitment.[66] In *Hamlet* he was trying (unconsciously perhaps) to recreate the experience of religious doubt *in its meaning* by the instrumentality of a revenge play whose only principle of form was the drift toward realism unlimited.[67] This principle, although defective, was not as defeating of artistic value as Eliot's strictures implied;[68] it succeeded when the vision to be unfolded was what Nietszche called "Apollonian," but proved faulty when the state of mind to be expressed was that of acedia, for then there could be no realistic objective correlative because the protagonist's feelings naturally exceeded the realistic facts in the situation. A symbolic objective correlative was needed, one that in painting might be called "non-representational."

Eliot does not spell all of this out in "Hamlet and his Problems," but if we take that essay in conjunction with later ones, something such as I have described may be seen taking shape in his mind. In talking about Shakespeare, as in talking about Blake, Eliot may well have been talking to himself. If *Hamlet* is an artistic failure, as Eliot asserts, then so is "The Love Song of J. Alfred Prufrock." Prufrock's intensities of response to the coffee-spoon circuit are in excess of the facts as they appear. In these two essays, Eliot is pointing out two directions the poet in a dry age must be wary of taking. When the depth has departed from communal life, the artist ought not to try to convert the community. And when the poet himself is in the grip of the demon of doubt, he ought not to attempt to force a formless realism to express his emotion.

If these are the remedial measures that Eliot forbad himself to take, what positive measures could he endorse? In approaching the third phase of Eliot's criticism, the prescriptive, we need to grant that at the root of the literary ailment was the malfeasance of the metaphysician *manqué* and that the cure had to start at the ground. A poet had first to re-establish his metaphysical standpoint. Then he had to find an appropriate form for an arid period. Finally he had to find a point of contact with the contemporary mind at a place where it met the mind of the past. The essay that lets us see how Eliot attempted to do these three things is the "Lettre d'Angleterre" (1923) in *La Nouvelle Revue Française* where Eliot names F. H. Bradley, Henry James, and Sir James Frazer as his "masters." [69] That essay needs to be taken in conjunction, of course, with several earlier ones, especially those on Ben Jonson, Henry James, and James Joyce. "Poetry of design" is the terminological memento of this phase of Eliot's therapy.

The singularity of a young poet's naming a metaphysician as a "master" influence on his work needs to be taken account of if we are to interpret correctly the somewhat cryptic announcement of that influence that Eliot makes in the "Lettre d'Angleterre." The cryptic attitude calls attention to the fact that the poet is gratefully acknowledging, not receipt of ideas, but the development of a sensibility. The philosopher has enabled the poet to preserve what Blake had—naked vision—and then has provided what Blake had not—a tradition. If we bear in mind that Bradley's philosophizing is an instrument for cleaning the springs of consciousness, we comprehend why Eliot speaks of receiving everything and nothing from Bradley, and expresses gratitude for being left in a state of "bewitched despair." Does this not seem to mean that the poet came to the metaphysician in a state of mind where he was unable to enjoy any form of spiritual life except that of thinking? What aroused the poet's interest was that he found the philosopher sitting in the same wilderness that he himself was in. What evoked the disciple's gratitude was that this master required nothing but a thoroughgoing skepticism; no water from exhausted wells, no capacity to see airborne mirages was needed. [70] The discipline consisted of learning to pay attention to the broken images in the desert. But by that discipline the consummate metaphysician purified the poet's sense of an ultimate reality without which poetry is a game.

Thus, Bradley's dialectic freed the poet's standpoint, recovered for him a traditional metaphysical sensibility, and left him free to do the poet's work in an uncongenial age. It provided, moreover, a hint of a poetic method. If every appearance in life points to an absolute order which is the meaning of the appearance, then we can begin to take an absorbed interest in the negative forms of human activity. A poet, incapable of anything but thinking, can record observations of the moral life of the living dead, convinced that hollow men live in the Absolute too. An ultimate reality moves in their whispers and such movement is the one right subject for a dry poet in a dry season. "Preludes" (1910–11) looks like a good illustration of the way Bradley's dialectic might be applied to a poem. The quotidian urban life points perpetually to a transcendant reality that the "eyes assured of certain certainties" deny.

From seeing a poetic method in a philosopher's mode of thought to examining the procedures of the past for an unsuspected tradition is but a step. I see Eliot taking it in his essays on Marlowe (1919), Jonson (1919), and Dryden (1921). "Ben Jonson," as a matter of fact, looks like a companion piece to "Hamlet and his Problems." If "Hamlet" is a statement of what not to do when caught in the dark night of the soul, "Ben Jonson" is, perhaps, a statement of what might be done. "Poetry of design," "poetry of the surface"—a poetry that is "so very conscious and deliberate that we must look with eyes alert to the whole before we apprehend the significance of any part," a poetry which uses surface details to create worlds "which are like systems of non-Euclidean geometry," a poetry whose logic "illuminates the actual world" by giving us a "new point of view from which to inspect it" [71]— this is Eliot's prescription for himself. In an arid period like ours—so I see Eliot's ideas going together—poetry of the surface enables us to be tough and realistic without being victims of "realism unlimited." We can keep our wits about us; we can start with a human brain in a human environment.[72] We can take the facts of quotidian life as they come to us—smell of cooking, noise of typewriter [73]—and by a kind of montage achieve designs that reach directly the emotions of art.[74] We thus bypass attempts to reproduce ordinary emotional responses of actual life.[75] Ben Jonson's "two-dimensional" art is a "part of our literary inheritance craving further expression." [76]

Although I may be wrong, Eliot's ideas on intellectual poetry do not always seem intelligible without the presence of a specific ontological outlook. When, using a shifting vocabulary, he describes the method without describing the outlook, he is apt to leave readers perplexed. What keeps the poetic designs of a "pure intellectual" (like Jean Bosschère to whom Eliot, in the *Egoist*, October 1917, enthusiastically applies the phrase) from being arbitrary? What keeps Ezra Pound's historical method from dumping bric-a-brac on a reader? [77] What is the point of Joyce's juxtaposing past and present in the exercise of a "mythical method"? [78] (Eliot would have answered, I suppose, that his remarks were meant to apply to artists who were artists and to be interpreted by readers who were intelligent.)

I seem to see what Eliot is driving at when I find him placing Henry James next to F. H. Bradley as his second "master". What Eliot says about James's fictional characters resembles what he says about Ben Jonson's. They are real, but not realistic. They derive their peculiar reality (by contrast with other authors' fictional people who sometimes seem assembled in the same novel by accident) by the way they fit together to make a total design. But here Eliot clears up what he does not clarify elsewhere, the source of the vitality in James's designs. James's form is the result of his vision of an "ideal society," a vision so exigent that it compelled him to achieve exact expression.[79] The "ideal society" that Eliot speaks of must be the same as the Josiah Royce *community*; it is a metaphysical entity, and now I know where I am, or where Eliot is. If F. H. Bradley reveals the "still point" (*Burnt Norton*, V), then James shows the way to the "still point" (a downward way). Bradley rehabilitates the final cause of literary expression and James the formal.

If we come now to Eliot's third "master" and inquire what he contributed to the poet's rehabilitation, we may almost guess that he redeemed, for purposes of art, the efficient cause. This, at any rate, is what I shall argue. The artist's problem in an arid age is how, without falsifying the material that is his *given*, to move that material toward art. In an urban, scientific culture, the problem is especially difficult because the eyes that fix things in a formulated phrase have already pinned just about everything living to the wall. What Frazer does is to pin up for attention facts drawn from pre-scientific, pre-urban societies widely separated in space and time. Frazer's facts are impressively factual so that they suit contemporary ways of seeing. But these facts embody what primitive communities did ritualistically in interim situations, in those seasons of the year when the life of the community, or the primitive sense of the community of all life, was threatened. These facts, therefore, do something to our eyes. What they do, Eliot says, is provide a glimpse of the human soul from a new angle, a glimpse into the abyss as valuable as that provided by Freud and perhaps in the long run more useful.[80] What Eliot means, perhaps, is that both Frazer and Freud provide insights into the real bases of psychic life, as opposed to the apparent foundations. But Freud's principles of interpretation forced him to reduce psychic phenomena to what they come from, physiological foundations, whereas Frazer, having no conceptual framework, left the way open for an interpretation of his data in terms of what psychic life moves toward, a spiritual life.

What Frazer's *Golden Bough* offers the poet is a point where factual past and factual present meet. He provides the point where Bradley's dialectic can operate, not on abstractions, but upon concrete events. Or this is what I take to be the manner of the "mythic method" that Eliot hails in his essay on Joyce's *Ulysses*. Frazer's facts suggest that archaic and contemporary behaviour are already juxtaposed in contemporary consciousness, and that a poet can further refine the juxtapositions, not necessarily to disparage the latter and glorify the former as is sometimes supposed, but to disclose a ground of identity and to reveal the presence of a third entity, a metaphysical community in all men.[81] That Frazer himself had no such vision of an ideal society as Eliot has enhances his value. His compendium of human folly, Eliot's phrase, provides a record of earlier man's misguided efforts to contain and control a life beyond life (which is my interpretation of what he means). These efforts were misguided because they were magical. But set against our own unconscious magical rites, they may sensitize us to our own folly.

The pragmatic test of Eliot's critical theories was *The Waste Land,* the poem which I should perhaps be interpreting but am not. (In the Appendix, I try to speak of the design of the work; but that design does not seem to me to quite reach the public domain. It is Eliot's *Hamlet.*) I turn to *Burnt Norton* for illustration of Eliot's poetry of design. Although difficult, it is a public poem, the first of a series in which the discipline that the poet had won for himself in private is brought to bear on the crises of a world.

4 BURNT NORTON

> "In the tale here presented, the dust of our natural divisions is stirred into new life."—Josiah Royce, The Problem of Christianity, I, 211.

T. S. ELIOT once (in his first essay on Milton) drew a distinction between the goodness and greatness of poetry, a distinction that we seem to understand until we think about it. If a poem could be great, and yet not good, the "greatness" would have to come either from materials which, in some other context, had had significance, or come from the artist's ingenuity, which in the context of the "poem" would have to be judged misplaced. Either way there would be neither greatness nor goodness. Poems have integrity or do not have integrity, and if they do not, neither the materials nor the ingenuity are artistic and there is nothing to call great. What might be spoken of as the greatness of a poem, in separation from its goodness, is the significance of the act that the poem makes.

Adopting this point of view, we might say that whatever greatness Burnt Norton has (as distinct from its goodness, which is the subject of discussion in the subsequent essay) it has as a defense of poetry. We might say this provided we remember that poetry is something that only a literary critic would feel in need of defending and only a poet who is also a philosopher is capable of defending. A really successful defense, like a defense of one's questioned virtue or patriotism or piety, is achievable only by an act.

Grant that we may talk this way, then *Burnt Norton* is one of the great defenses of poetry in the English language. It is much superior to Sidney's, who seemed too young fully to grasp what the issue was, and better than Shelley's, who wrote a very great defense, indeed, but had not matured sufficiently to recognize the ambiguities of good and evil in art. (It is hard to know for sure whether this is or is not true of the man who wrote *Prometheus Unbound* and *Adonais*.) Nevertheless, the virtue of *Burnt Norton* as a defense of poetry is that it is written by a poet who grants in advance (as neither Sidney nor Shelley do) the validity of Plato's indictment of imitative poetry: that art tends to usurp the place of knowledge and reality in men's lives, and that when it does it is ruinous to the mind and the character. Most people, Eliot once said, do not live in the real world but in a quasi-real world of second-rate literature. This statement shows that the poet had assimilated Plato's point. Eliot's defensive tactics are to show that the soul which falls by the imagination rises by the imagination and that the way up and the way down are the same way.

If we look at the work that Eliot was doing in the five-year period between *Ash-Wednesday* (1930) and *Burnt Norton* (1935), we find that a recurrent theme in his thought is the use of poetry and the misuse of poetry. In the Charles Eliot Norton Lectures that Eliot delivered at Harvard during the winter of 1932–33, and published as *The Use of Poetry and the Use of Criticism,* Eliot seemed to be leading his hearers to an overwhelming conclusion which he quoted from Jacques Maritain, *Art and Scholasticism:* "It is a deadly error to expect poetry to provide the super-substantial nourishment of man." The poet added: "Mr. Maritain is a theologian as well as a philosopher and you may be sure that when he says 'deadly error' he is in deadly earnest."

In the Page Barbour Lectures delivered at the University of Virginia in 1933 and published as *After Strange Gods,* Eliot is concerned (among other things) "with the intrusion of the *diabolic* into modern literature," with that "positive power for evil working through the human agency," with evil that "may operate through men of genius of the most excellent character." These lectures are repellent because of the atmosphere they generate of a Salem witchcraft trial. The Eliot soul seems so bent on serving its maker that it almost joins the devil's party without realizing it. But the lectures are important background for *Burnt Norton*.

Eliot's preoccupation with the use and misuse of imagination, with the evil potential in the aesthetic, goes back to his beginning. But the spiritual crisis recorded in *Ash-Wednesday* perhaps intensified his Kierkegaard-like awareness of the dangers of a poet's vocation. At the end of *Ash-Wednesday*, the poet-protagonist is found praying to the guardian Lady "Blessèd sister, holy mother, spirit of the fountain, spirit of the garden,/ Suffer us not to mock ourselves with falsehood," but the poem begins and ends in a dilemma: The poet seems to be in a position where he dare not *not* use that talent which is death to hide and dare not not renounce it. He can move neither forward nor back. *Burnt Norton* rescues him from this jeopardy of the will.

ii

Burnt Norton shows how Eliot's "intellectual" poetry may try the patience of an educated reader. A title names a place no one needs ever to have heard of; two untranslated Greek epigraphs follow, observations of an Ionian philosopher philosophers call "the dark"; thereafter are eight verses on time, prosaic as any in English literature. What is the effect? A reader who finds ignorance intolerable because it makes him feel guilty cannot continue until he discovers what the title signifies, what the epigraphs say, and whose ideas on time are being expressed. When told that "Burnt Norton" designates an English manor house at Ebrington in Gloucestershire near Chipping Camden where Eliot sojourned in the summer of 1934,[1] that the first epigraph has been rendered: "Although the Law of Reason (*logos*) is common, the majority of people live as though they had an understanding (wisdom) of their own," and the second: "The way upward and downward are one and the same." [2] and that the reflections on time are perhaps from Henri Bergson (whose lectures Eliot attended in Paris in the winter of 1911, finding his *durée réelle* "not final") [3] or from F. H. Bradley (whose *Appearance and Reality* Eliot purchased at the Harvard Co-operative in 1913) [4]—when advised of all this, the reader is apt to be more unsettled than when he halted his reading. Having left the dramatic orbit of the poem to raise some questions, he loses the principle of progression that will unify his scholarship. An illiterate man, one for whom Eliot once said that he wanted to write,[5] might perhaps have fared better. For him the title would name a place where a story started, the epigraphs are texts, and the voice is that of a man in trouble talking to himself. For an illiterate person, speech begins in men feeling and doing something, and for Aristotle poetry begins there too.

The interpreter of Eliot's poetry might well simulate the attitudes of the illiterate and make believe that he is in a theatre. *Burnt Norton* is the play to be given. The epigraphs are mottoes over the proscenium; they cover (though in a foreign tongue) almost every play the mind of man may devise; the cogitations on time are rhetorical; [6] like Hamlet's opening soliloquy, they define the way the protagonist sees himself; as for the story, it is the familiar one of a city dweller's vacation, a plot so familiar that the poet does not tell it; the theme is "paradise regained."

To take *Burnt Norton* as a play is not pretense; the structure of the poem is dramatic,[7] not discursive; when we see the poet as a protagonist and participate in his struggle, we follow the sequences. The dramatic action is primary. We must get it first. Most readers' difficulties with the poem are due rather to timidity of imagination than to inadequacy of erudition.

Nevertheless, the context of Eliot's action is the real reality, and before we try to elucidate *Burnt Norton* as philosophic poetry, we might consider briefly several metaphoric devices Eliot uses for implying the ultimate aspect of the action. The plot is the familiar story of the city dweller's vacation, and although it may seem farcical, the farce is serious, and the metaphor of going on a vacation, like the metaphor of going to the hospital in *East Coker*, or going on a journey in *Dry Salvages*, or going to the stake in *Little Gidding*, has extended implications. Going on a vacation is an expressive act, and what it expresses is partially recognized when we remember that *Burnt Norton* is the "air" quartet. "Air" signifies in Eliot's work the world of human activity. Air is the world of words, therefore of thoughts, and so of poetry and science. Air is between the sun (ultimate reality) and water (life) and earth (matter). Air, therefore, is the state of human freedom and place of human tragedy: here human beings take possession for themselves of the other elements and so actualize their estrangement from the real reality, transforming in the process, earth into dust, water into fog, or cloud, and sunlight into flicker. In air, human beings can *be* for themselves. The specific *hamartia* (tragic flaw) which underlies *Burnt Norton*, therefore, is man's unbelief, symbolically expressed by the action of going on vacation. The act expresses the human desire and power to take possession of spiritual life without being at-one with that spirit. It is peculiarly the poet's *hamartia*; at the same time the poet's missing of the mark is but a specialization of every man's urge while being in a condition of unbelief to enjoy the fruits of spiritual activity in separation from the ultimate source of these experiences. We could name the poet's *hamartia* "aestheticism," though that term may be too restrictive.

The demon of aestheticism, nevertheless, appears repeatedly in Eliot's work. In the 1917 poems, the sufferings of the young man are those of a spirit trapped in a world of air, a world where all the values are aridly aesthetic or intellectual. (The women come and go talking of Michaelangelo or of Chopin.) The knowledge that Gerontion condemns as apparently beyond the range of forgiveness is the aestheticizing of the Word made flesh. The climax of the first movement of *The Waste Land* is the recognition on the part of the poet that he himself is a *hypocrite lecteur* and the first step in his redemption must be the avoidance of resurrecting his dead life for the wrong reason (i.e. to make "art"). The climax of *Ash-Wednesday*, as I see it, is a horrified recognition that after, by virtue of the goodness of the Lady, he has realized a spiritual rebirth and been restored to his art, he finds himself tempted to estimate the profit and loss involved in the use of spiritual realities as material for art. *Burnt Norton* is the end of a long struggle, the final exorcising of the demon of the aesthetic.

We may wonder what is the precise relation of the struggle which is *Burnt Norton* to the struggle in the criticism and the struggle in the dissertation. The relation is oblique but essential. The death of air which constitutes the problem of the protagonist, has two forms: it is the death of the aesthetic, the sights and echoes which inhabit air, and the death of the universal, the corridors or paths which structure air. The push of the poem is to recommit the poet to a valid absolute, not identified with either the aesthetic or the universal, and yet expressed by both. In terms of the criticism, the aim is to reintegrate the poet's sensibility by finding, largely by a labor of intelligence, a formula that sets down all that he feels in a situation where his feelings are largely negative. I would like now to attempt an elucidation of *Burnt Norton* as *philosophical poetry*.

iii

Burnt Norton, Section I, consists of two scenes set in strong contrast, something we notice if we visualize them. The division is marked by a break in the versification. Scene 1 is set in a dim light, inside, in the passageways of the manor house; Scene 2 is set outside in full sunlight, in the rose garden. In the interior scene, movement takes place mainly inside the poet's head; despite the footfalls, I get the impression of physical immobility;

the ideas, however, go round and round and the end of their circling is despair. But in the rose garden, the movement seems physical, an actual circular dance, even though the dancers are only in the poet's imagination. The climax of that movement is ecstasy. The two scenes illustrate the "law" of the epigraph (the way up and the way down are one and the same way). If we miss the point of them we may miss the unfolding pattern in the rest of the poem. Materially, the two scenes are so different (dry thoughts in the first, intense feelings in the second) that interpretation must work differently on each. In Scene 1, we must ask: What feelings prompt these thoughts? In Scene 2, What ideas reveal the meaning of these feelings? A single canto of the *Divine Comedy*, Eliot once said, may compress as much meaning as a play of Shakespeare.[8] Eliot in *Burnt Norton*, Section I, seems aiming at a Dantean concentration, and forty-eight lines of verse may require extended commentary.

Scene 1 begins in the midst of things. What has already happened? The poet left London (this we may safely infer since in Section III he returns to London) and he did so (here imagination is needed) for reasons familiar to vacationers—to escape from a "place of disaffection" to a place where life seems "substantial and simplified."[9] The poet has discovered in the place of freedom that there is no freedom. Standing in a dim light, he hardly need tell us that he feels more a prisoner of time's corridor than ever.

Eliot is a master of right beginnings. The opening lines here that seem prosaic to Karl Shapiro[10] are unique in Eliot's work. In no other major poem has he used a tone so toneless. He might have made it by scraping his legs together.[11] The sound does not last long. By line eleven, there is the sound of personal emotion. But up to that point, the poet *is* a dry head. If we take his speech as we do a soliloquy, we are introduced directly to the mind of one, like Harry Monchensey, who feels that he has lost the possibility of possibility.[12] The first two words express the trouble. Nowhere else does he use the phrase

"time present." The phrase involves a contradiction since
a present really present is not temporal. His use of the
phrase implies that he has no real present. His "now,"
the center of freedom and being, is for him merely an
abstract point in a line of points stretching from the past
into the future. Or, to adopt Sartre's comment [13] on
Faulkner, the Eliot protagonist rides like a man in an
open car looking backward: he sees a past but no real
present or future.

The poet's struggle in Scene 1 might be thought of as
three unsuccessful attempts to adapt himself to "time
present." A rhythm is established: three lines followed by
two lines, three lines that express a mind more or less
going in a circle, two lines that show a mind knocking at
an unresponsive center. The lines are ambiguous, but, as
I read them, the first three lines define the problem—the
time-scape wherein there is no real present or free future,
only a recurrent past.

> Time present and time past
> Are both perhaps present in time future,
> And time future contained in time past.

I see in this the despair of Harry Monchensey: "O God,
man, the things that are going to happen/ Have already
happened," [14] or of the Chorus of Aunts and Uncles:

> I am afraid of all that has happened, and of all
>   that is to come;
> Of the things to come that sit at the door, as if
>   they had been there always.
> And the past is about to happen, and the future
>   was long since settled.
> And the wings of the future darken the past, the
>   beak and claws have desecrated
> History. [15]

As in every play, the beginning is pregnant with all that is
to happen, but we do not see until the end that the
plague confronting Oedipus or the love-test facing Lear's
daughters is the form destiny has taken. So here: the end-

less corridor is the poet's destiny made visible for his recognition and for the reversal of his intentions.

The next two lines flicker with hope and despair.

> *If all time is eternally present*
> *All time is unredeemable.*

The third appearance of the key work *present* is notable. For if all time is to be *time present,* then all time is just hopeless: no future can be any better than the past. We cannot redeem the time. Yet if we cannot redeem it, perhaps in "time present" we can find a point of rest. Is there a flicker of hope in this despair? Lines 6–8 circle such a false still point.

> *What might have been is an abstraction*
> *Remaining a perpetual possibility*
> *Only in a world of speculation.*

Again the lines are ambiguous. But the rhetoric of dismissal can be taken as offering reassurance. If what might have been exists only in speculation, then there is no point in either yearning for what we did not get or feeling guilty for failing to get it. The poet now refocuses this center and the "hope" glows brighter momentarily.

> *What might have been and what has been*
> *Point to one end, which is always present.*

This is the paradoxical happiness that Keats complimented the lover on the Grecian Urn for enjoying. Whether we fulfill our intentions or not, our fulfillment is always present in our heads at least. Why repine? The poet circles this point again and for the first time the language grows specific as the poet approaches the world he lives in as distinct from the world he thinks in.

> *Footfalls echo in the memory*
> *Down the passage which we did not take*
> *Towards the door we never opened.*

These interesting lines (11–13)—note how time present is an echo of time past that reaches toward time future— place the poet in the hell of phantasmal solitude [16] that

Harcourt-Reilly speaks of in *The Cocktail Party*. The
crumb of comfort implicit in lines 4–5 and 9–10 turns
out to be nothing to live on. The poet has come to the
state Pascal describes: "For in fact, if man had never been
corrupt, he would enjoy in his innocence both truth and
happiness with assurance; and if man had always been
corrupt, he would have no idea of truth or bliss. But,
wretched as we are, and more so than if there were no
greatness in our condition, we have an idea of happiness
and cannot reach it." [17]

The lines that follow do interesting things. Lines 14–15
represent the center. For the first time the "circling"
triple lines run over and reach the "centering" double
lines, and for the first time the double line itself is broken.
The effect is peculiar.

> *Into the rose garden. My words echo*
> *Thus, in your mind.*

The "rose garden" is not the specious center that "time
present" is, but the "eternal in time." And the woman ad-
dressed becomes the corridor toward and door into the
rose garden. The poet here projects himself outside of
himself into the woman. He identifies himself by becoming the echoes in her, somewhat as Harry identifies himself in *The Family Reunion* with "the old house/ With
the noxious smell and the sorrow before morning." [18] But
centering himself as echoes in the woman's mind, the
poet, though close to realization of his condition, is not
fully stripped of the illusion of hope. To be able to say
"My words echo/ Thus, in your mind" is to have a kind
of career, that of a ruined lover.[19] But lines 16–18 evapo-
rate this illusion. I would like to see the break in the text
as an emphatic way of marking the poet's climactic realization of his separation from real being. By becoming
echoes in the mind of the person who might have been
the door to the garden, the poet emphasizes not only his
futility but culpability. Words stirring dust on a bowl of
rose leaves (note the centering image of the bowl) would
seem to be like the spectres of desire haunting a body

once capable of love but now no longer so. If the poet is thought of as a protagonist, and if he is the protagonist-as-poet (creator of echoes and images), his identification with futile and culpable forms of expression is a serious rejection of himself as a poet. In coming from the city of disaffection to Burnt Norton, the poet has, it would seem, come to the "jolly corner," that "loop in time" where he has to see himself as he is.[20] The opening of *Burnt Norton* could be seen conforming to the type of crisis that Nietzsche described as the "jeopardy of the will," the point of nausea where the "birth of tragedy" occurs.[21] Or, to use a third illustration, he has come to a place where he can "go neither back nor forward." [22]

The dramatic context of the second scene is the "nothingness" that the poet reaches in the first scene. He responds by entering the garden and being drawn toward ecstasy. The logic would seem to be something like this: the poet's vacation expressed a hope grounded in despair, and arrival at the destination merely uncovered the despair; but the poet's despair in the corridors of Burnt Norton is grounded in an ecstatic background that is always present, in idea at least, if not in fact. The movement into the rose garden is a way of uncovering the ecstatic background.

We have to keep two things in mind when we wonder what the journey into the rose garden means. First the journey is a decisive act; the poet at the outset puts the question to us twice whether we shall go. When he says: "Into our first world," he answers his question with an act. What the poet wills frames the scene. The whole scene is the objectification of an intention. Second, the poet is *given* something: at this point it is enough to say that he is given a sequence of visionary events that gradually take possession of him. To contemplate the meaning of Scene 2 we have not only to feel the poet's intention; this is relatively easy; we have also to think what each phase of what is given him means. This is not so easy. We have to "think with our feelings," [23] which means that we have to give the details of this section the kind of attention a lawyer gives his brief.[24]

The poet's intention is not without ambiguity; the end in view changes as Scene 2 progresses, and one of the chief reading problems here is how to interpret whatever is designated by the pronoun, "they." When the poet says (lines 19–20) "Other echoes/ Inhabit the garden. Shall we follow?" his pursuit seems directed toward "other echoes," echoes, that is, other than those of our corridor-bound feet, echoes of what might have been, echoes of freedom and happiness. When the bird says, "Quick, . . . find them, find them./ Round the corner" the poet's objective still seems to be echoes, though there may be a doubt. When the poet says, "Through the first gate,/ Into our first world, shall we follow/ The deception of the thrush?" the doubt develops. What is the deception? And when having launched ourselves into our first world, we look about us, what we intuit first is, "There they were," and the impression is that they are presences not echoes, even though "moving without pressure over the dead leaves" is something either echoes or presences might do. For the rest of the scene, if "they" are echoes "they" are echoes the way ghosts are. In the action that follows inside the garden, "they" play a fateful role, appearing twice on the stroke of the seventh line (lines 25 and 32) and then, somewhat anticlimactically, once on the eighth. Their positions with respect to us mark the stages of the action: "There they were, dignified, invisible" (in front of us); "There they were as our guests, accepted and accepting" (at our side); "And they were behind us, reflected in the pool" (both behind and before us). Hearing "them" seems to be the prelude to entrance into the rose garden; seeing "them" reflected in the pool seems to be the prelude to expulsion from the garden. Who or what are "they?" "They," I think, are essentially mysterious and any exegesis of them that destroys the mystery mars the poetry. But taking them for the moment simply in relation to the poet's act, "they" are what the poet, in the corridor, wishes *we* could have been. "They" are the selves we think we might have been. In the corridor "they" exist as echoes; inside the first gate "they" exist as something else—not echoes, nor presences—but what?

When Celia Coplestone in *The Cocktail Party* falls out of love with Edward she apologizes to him because what she had loved in him was, she says, something she had projected on him, something that she desperately wanted to exist.[25] When Celia says this she is already half outside the gate of the rose garden, and the object of her aspiration is an "echo." But while under the spell of her infatuation, the echo is not a mere echo, but a presence, yet not a presence where Celia locates it (in Edward Chamberlayne's person.) We might therefore interpret the poet's temptation in the corridor to find "them" as every man's impulse to find by sexual love what Celia calls that "new person us." [26] To our corridor-bound selves, "they" seem "real," but to believe this is to be deluded by the deception of the thrush. Some readers have interpreted "them" as the children we hear at the end of the scene.[27] But at the start of the scene, the poet has told us precisely how "they" are experienced, and I would say that "they" are not children until we are at the point of expulsion. But we cannot say all that "they" are until we scan the scene as a whole. At the beginning what is important is to place them in the context of the poet's act.

But the ambiguousness of the poet's intention leads us forward to the poet's act, and we discover as we might expect that his act is many-sided. The poet is doing at least four things at once. First, he is literally going for a walk in the rose garden at Burnt Norton. Second, he is following the deception of the thrush, which is to say, he is permitting himself to live a moment in his life as if he were writing a poem. Third, he is re-enacting something crucial in his own and every person's life, an initiation into the mystery of sexual experience. Fourth, he is re-enacting the myth of paradise lost. The poet does in these twenty-five lines what Harry Monchensey laments cannot be done: he lives on several planes at once and speaks with several voices.[28]

The sequence of tenses in Scene 2 underlines the multiformity of the action. So long as the poet stands in the corridor he uses the present tense. ("Footfalls echo. . . .

My words echo.") At the start of Scene 2 the poet continues to use the present tense. ("Other echoes/ Inhabit the garden.") When the poet weighs entering the garden, he uses, understandably, a future tense. ("Shall we follow?") The passage into the rose garden is still ahead of us in time. But at this point the employment of tenses becomes somewhat peculiar. The thrush speaks in the past tense. ("Quick, *said* the bird, find them, find them.") The past tense would seem to convey the idea that what the bird commands is an echo of what it once commanded in the past. The poet's decision, however, to enter our first world is so immediately of the present that the poet does not even use a verb. ("Into our first world.") Volition and fulfillment are simultaneous. What happens in the garden, nevertheless, is firmly planted in past time. ("There they *were*. . . . And the bird *called*. . . . the roses/ *Had* the look . . . So we *moved* . . . And the lotus *rose*"). The expulsion from the garden ("Go, *said* the bird") is in past tense and we do not come back to the present until the final three lines of the scene, spoken by the poet outside the garden. The insistent use of past tense seems to emphasize that "we" are re-enacting an association with "them" that either did occur for the speaker with someone else (but not with "you"), or that might have occurred as in the *The Family Reunion:*

I was not there, you were not there, only our phantasms
And what did not happen is as true as what did happen.[29]

The interweaving of present, future, and past tenses leads me to think that at least six characters may be involved in this multilateral action. There is We no. 1, the poet and his mistress, who never opened the door into the rose garden, but are doing so now by deliberate imaginative act. Next there is "they" whom We no. 1 are presently in pursuit of, Adam and Eve, mythically speaking, or what We no. 1 might have been had we entered the rose garden. Finally there is We no. 2, the *we* that in some past time encountered "them," danced with "them," and saw "them" reflected in the pool, and whose encounter, dance, and vision We no. 1 are re-enacting in such fashion as to begin the redemption of all six "characters." If this seems unnecessarily complicated, we may look at *Family Reunion* where we see that the Erinyes that Harry is in flight from seem to involve at least three ghosts.[30]

The action that occurs in Scene 2, as must be obvious, is a good example of "intellectual" poetry, and no literal-minded statement can do justice to it. Before analyzing the dramatic progression, we probably need to give heed to the way Eliot has used literary echoes and iconographic images to place for the reader the unfolding action in a context of recurrent art experiences and prevalent interpretations.

The literary echoes are numerous; for the most part, I can restrict myself to such as have been detected. In general, Eliot's literary allusions are to tell us that the experiences that we are here experiencing have been experienced by such and such poets in the past who interpreted their experiences in such and such terms, and these interpretations do or do not coincide with the ultimate interpretation offered here.

The first echo that I note nobody else has heard, and I speak of it with some hesitation. Nevertheless, Eliot's thrush plays an important role in the drama of the garden: he appears to inspire us to enter the garden, to encourage us to join the dance, and then to expel us. We would expect Eliot to place so important a character in a frame of interpretation, even though there is reason to believe (from "Marina," and Section V of *The Waste Land*) that the thrush may be a purely private symbol drawn from the poet's personal experience. Nevertheless, behind Eliot's thrush in *Burnt Norton* I seem to hear the sound of Walt Whitman's thrush in "When Lilacs Last in the Dooryard Bloom'd." The two birds have points in common. Both are symbols of the poetic "demon" in life. Both are located on the frontier between time and eternity, life and death. Both are liberators and redeemers. Whitman's thrush releases him from the "cloud" that holds Whitman powerless at the opening of the poem;

Eliot's thrush releases him from the corridor. Both birds thus lead their poets to a reconciliation of seemingly irreconcilable forces in life. Yet by stressing the "deception of the thrush," Eliot qualifies Whitman's romantic and somewhat sentimental deification of the poet. Whitman declares that he is moving toward the thrush in the swamp and that all is well; but he never takes us into the swamp to see how well things are going down there. Eliot's bird is eager but limited in intelligence; he is strong on luring people into transcendental situations which he does not understand and cannot control and then ejecting them when they fail to measure up. Eliot, in short, makes it clear that though art may be a means to redemption it may also be a means to damnation and that something more than Ariel is needed to transform Caliban.

Nevertheless, if the Whitman allusion is valid, Eliot is, through it, offering one interpretation of what the excursion into the rose garden means. It is "poetry," in Plato's sense of the word (*The Symposium*), an effort to join together being and nonbeing.

The first gate and the first world that are the setting for our first encounter with "them" constitute for some interpreters [31] an obvious allusion to Milton's account of Adam and Eve in the Garden. The line (25) "There they were, dignified, invisible," reinforces the impression. What Eliot wished to signify he had declared perhaps in his remarks on Milton's Adam and Eve:

> These are not a man and woman such as any we know: if they were, they would not be Adam and Eve. They are the original *Man* and *Woman*, not types, but prototypes. They have the general characteristics of men and women, such that we can recognize in the temptation and fall, the first motions of the faults and virtues, the abjection and the nobility, of all their descendants. They have ordinary humanity to the right degree, and yet are not, and should not be, ordinary mortals.[32]

Because of the role "they" play in "Burnt Norton," the Miltonic allusion seems of considerable significance. "They" are not merely the ideal selves that the poet and his mistress might have been, they are "first parents"—

not persons, but prototypes. By making them invisible, Eliot has corrected the Miltonic tendency to make Adam and Eve too concrete, too literally flesh and blood. Even so, the Milton reference can be bad for comprehension of Eliot's "them" unless we remember that meeting "them" is in the rose garden, a mythic world where the child is father of the man and nothing may be taken literally. Once we do identify Eliot's "them" with Milton's Adam and Eve, we probably should go to a theologian like Paul Tillich for clarification of "Adam and Eve." [33] He emphasizes that "our first parents" must not be interpreted as actual persons who lived in a specific place and whose fall was an event that happened once upon a time. Adam must be understood first as a symbol of *essential* man, man, that is, in unity with God; second as a symbol of the transition from essence to existence, a symbol of man actualizing his freedom in such a way as to estrange himself from God. The "fall of Adam" must be taken as a symbol of the human situation universally, the universal destiny of estrangement that concerns every man. Eliot's handling of this symbolic aspect of "them" seems very careful. When We no. 2 meet them, it is We no. 2 that are innocent and "they" who are "fallen." The movement of "we" and "they" back to the center of the garden restores "them" to unity with God (the heart of light) and deprives "us" of innocence. Thus "they" are the transition for "Us no. 2" from dreaming innocence to knowledge and actualized freedom.

In portraying the transition from rose garden to boxwood circle, Eliot uses two allusions that others have noted, and that are interesting examples of the way Eliot is apt to convert, or invert, the work of his predecessors. Once inside the gate of our first world, we contemplate in silence "them" moving without pressure over the dead leaves for three lines. Then the bird sounds again (lines 28–29):

> And the bird called, in response to
> The unheard music hidden in the shrubbery.

The "unheard music" in this context looks like a pointed reference to Keats's "Ode on a Grecian Urn":

> *Heard melodies are sweet, but those unheard*
> *Are sweeter; therefore, ye soft pipes, play on;*
> *Not to the sensual ear, but, more endear'd,*
> *Pipe to the spirit ditties of no tone:*

A moment later when the poet observes (lines 30–31)

> *And the unseen eyebeam crossed, for the roses*
> *Had the look of flowers that are looked at*

we are intended perhaps to recollect John Donne's "The Extasie" where the lines

> *Our eye-beames twisted, and did thread*
> *Our eyes, upon one double string;*

express the kind of at-oneness exemplified by "them" in the rose garden.

If these allusions are in the poem, Eliot is perhaps employing them in three ways. First he uses them to consolidate the experience we are having, to suggest how well established in familiar works is the experience of ecstasy, the exodus of the soul from the body. Second, he is using them to suggest the directions the rose garden experience of love can take: upward in artistic sublimation with Keats, downward toward copulation with Donne. Third, he is using these allusions to suggest that the movement We no. 1 are making combines these movements and either up or down is the same way; both end in the drained pool of desolation which can be transfigured. This interpretation, though speculative, fits the pattern of action, and, what is more, explains what I take to be Eliot's ironic inversion of his poetic ancestors as he makes the movement from rose garden to boxwood circle. For Keats's "unheard" music becomes the incitement, not for sublimation, but for Donne's descent into the body.

Two other allusions seem to help us refine the vision: These are to Henry James's "The Jolly Corner" and "The Turn of the Screw." The reference to "The Jolly Corner" is evident (lines 21–22):

> *Quick, said the bird, find them, find them*
> *Round the corner.*

In *The Family Reunion* Eliot took pains to be explicit:

> *The man who returns will have to meet*
> *The boy who left. Round by the stables,*
> *In the coach-house, in the orchard,*
> *In the plantation, down the corridor*
> *That led to the nursery, round the corner*
> *Of the new wing, he will have to face him—*
> *And it will not be a very* jolly *corner.*
> *When the loop in time comes—and it does*
> *   not come for everybody—*
> *The hidden is revealed, and the spectres show*
> *   themselves.*[34]

"The Jolly Corner" makes us see that following "them" is not from lack of anything better to do, but from the compulsion to resurrect the unlived life; James's story also makes us realize that such an action is not without danger. I cannot be sure that "The Turn of the Screw" is being echoed in this part of *Burnt Norton;* I may be quite wrong; nevertheless, I sense a strong resemblance between the whole action of Eliot's Scene 2 and James's famous ghost story. The Eden of the rose garden at Burnt Norton seems similar to the Eden at Bly that James's governess enters; her encounter with the charming children, Miles and Flora, is like the poet's encounter with the ambiguous "them." They are both innocent and "fallen," and the innocent governess's meeting with them is filled with danger for them and her. As I read the story, it is a twentieth-century version of paradise lost, and the governess's adult (but unimaginative) efforts to resist evil [35] lead her to become the instrument through whom the children are lost. If the Milton allusion makes us aware of what we yearn for from time's corridor, and the Keats and Donne references make us aware of the dubiety of our erotic and aesthetic strategies for gaining possession of the good we are estranged from, the James allusion seems to make us aware of the necessary character of our pursuit, the ambivalent character of all value, and the need for self-knowledge if the pursuit is to avoid disaster.

More palpable than the literary echoes, and easier to interpret, the iconographic images Eliot uses mark the phases of our pursuit of "them" in the garden. I call such things as the corridor, rose garden, box circle, pool, lotus and so forth, iconographic images because not only are they symbols, but symbols that are meant to imply a certain frame of interpretation outside the poem. Ananda Coomaraswamy [36] has declared that Eliot's images are part of a universal symbolic vocabulary and those properly initiated may read it; possibly the imagery in *Burnt Norton* speaks more directly to the oriental than to the occidental mind. Eliot's imagery is still largely unexplored, and I shall do no more than arrange systematically what seem to be the obvious meanings of several iconographic signs. Thus we may see how these images demarcate what is happening as "we" move from corridor to "heart of light" and back to corridor.

The corridor: The soul's place of imprisonment; at one level this would be the body; at another it would be the whole of the material world. (See Eliot's use of the same image in *Family Reunion*.) [37]

The first gate: Consider the gate to the Garden of Adonis in Spenser's Third Book of the *Faerie Queen* through which souls of children pass into the world. (See Eliot's similar use in *Family Reunion*.) [38]

The Garden (as a whole): The place of unity and generation, as in Dante's Earthly Paradise. The point where natural and supernatural are not estranged.

The rose garden (one part of the garden): The place where roses grow, and this would mean a place of love where we meet persons through whom and in whom we glimpse what gives us ultimate meaning and being. In *Ash-Wednesday*, the single rose is now the garden where all loves end. ("They" appear in the rose garden; "we" don't join them until the boxwood maze.)

The box circle: the boxwood circle is another center of life, like the rose garden, but an evergreen one. I assume that most of Eliot's evergreens (the yew, the fir, etc.) are symbols of life that persists (unlike the rose) summer and winter. Thus life at the box circle is life that persists whether we are in love or not, self-conscious or not; this life would be a form of being shared with plant life.

The concrete pool (dry concrete): This is the third center in the garden, the grey one. It is "the last of earth left to discover" (*Little Gidding*). It seems to me to go with Eliot's bone imagery. If rose garden, box circle, and drained pool are all conditions known to lovers, then the drained pool would seem to be the condition of the lover when he recognizes that "No contact possible to flesh/ Allayed the fever of the bone" ("Whispers of Immortality"). What human love seeks is a life beyond life, a supernatural life. The pool is empty because this life has been lost in the living; if the concrete pool is a bone image, then the empty concrete is analogous to the condition of the bones in *Ash-Wednesday* after the leopards have done their work. It is that which had been contained in the bones which answers God.

The water: Springing not from earth, but descending from the sun, this is the water of spiritual life; this would be the water that issues from the light of the world and which quenches thirst eternally.

The lotus: The lotus (because it springs not from earth but from water), from remote times has symbolized the possibility of superhuman or divine life existing in the context of nature and yet unsullied by its context.[39] In Buddhist pictures it appears often at the hub of a wheel and signifies the one secure ground of human self-sufficiency—purity of motive, detachment from all desire for the fruits of action.[40]

The heart of light: This is the figure Eliot uses recurrently for the "real reality." (See *The Waste Land*, I, "Looking into the heart of light, the silence.")

The cloud: This is a traditional symbol for what separates man from God. It is St. Paul's "flesh." When Blake represents a child sitting *on* a cloud, that is a Christ emblem.

I doubt that a reader has to recognize the auditory and visual signals used to interpret the action. Even here, illiteracy has privileges and advantages. In the end, reading Scene 2 depends on seeing a specific dramatic progression that begins in the corridor when the poet hears echoes that inhabit the garden and asks, "Shall we follow?" The ensuing action has two sides: there is what the poet-protagonist intends here and now in the present; and there is what he is given as the objectification of his intention. The two correlate. "Sin is Behovely," Eliot states in *Little Gidding*, "but/ All shall be well, and/ All manner of thing shall be well/ . . . By the purification of the motive/ In the ground of our beseeching." His utterance could be taken as a key to what is happening in this scene. The ground of the poet's beseeching is the "heart of light," the love which is always present, but from which he is separated. The motive, the specific intention, that moves the poet to follow the echoes, to succumb to the deception of the thrush is the desire to know a spiritual condition without being it. The poet's decision to enter the rose garden is a repetition of the artist's *hamartia*. He has to do what he does (Sin is Behovely) just as Oedipus has to do what he does to meet the exigency of the plague in Thebes. But the dramatic progression will unfold a series of paradoxical fulfillments through which the poet-protagonist moves toward a purgation of the original motive.

As I see the structuring of Scene 2, the poet moves by virtue of his intention toward three conjunctions that involve three kinds of plenitude, each being a kind of life and a kind of death because each is partial. The movement in Scene 2 seems to contrast with that in Scene 1. In Scene 1, the movement was steadily toward three disjunctions, each of which brought a new sense of desolation.

The first conjunction in Scene 2 (lines 25–26) is with our first world, the rose circle. The particular plenitude involved is a heightened sensibility evidenced by power to feel "them":

> *There they were, dignified, invisible,*
> *Moving without pressure, over the dead leaves.*

The meeting with "them," however, is a complex event. We no. 1 (the loveless, the estranged), are re-encountering that moment in the past when We no. 2 (the innocent, the neophytes in love), first encountered "them" (the temptation symbols of the transition from dreaming innocence to existential estrangement). "Their" setting— the dead leaves—indicates that their summer is over, that their fall has already occurred, even though they have not yet been expelled. The "autumn heat" reinforces the impression that summer is over, that the sunlight and singing phase of love is past; heat (desire) is more predominant than light.

If we ask as to the logic of the setting, if we ask, that is, why the poet's intention at its first conjunction meets what it seeks, but meets it in an environment that denies the intention, all we can say is that the poet's original intention has a flawed quality. The intention is to pursue our real selves; but the intention is proof that a fall has already occurred.

The second conjunction is with "them" in the formal dance along the empty alley into the box circle. This event, like the first, is prepared for by the call of the bird. It, too, seems a complex occurrence. Contrast the second call of the bird (lines 28–29)

> *And the bird called, in response to*
> *The unheard music hidden in the shrubbery,*

with the first (lines 21–22)

> *Quick, said the bird, find them, find them*
> *Round the corner.*

We note that the deceptive bird is no longer mediating between us and "them," but between "them" and some pulse vibrating in the world of nature. What is the unheard music hidden in the shrubbery? Taking the facts in context, we might guess that it is some harmony which nature has got that "they" have not got, just as "they" as

echoes inhabiting the garden have a harmony which the
poet's footfalls echoing in the corridor have not yet got.
If we bear in mind that we are repeating (as estranged
adults) what We no. 2 did half-knowing in the past, the
unheard music marks, perhaps, the moment in an initiation into sexuality when as children we became aware of
some secret life of the spirit resident in nature, mysterious
and intriguing, but not yet actualized in us. The conjunction which occurs is the actualization of the child's latent
sexuality. The bird's second call signals a change in motivation from "find them" to what to do with them, which
is to penetrate what in "Murder in the Cathedral" is
called the "spiritual flesh of nature," the "animal powers
of spirit." [41] The auditory image with the Keatsian over-
tone sounds "time future." The visual image which immediately follows (lines 30–31)

> And the unseen eyebeam crossed, for the roses
> Had the look of flowers that are looked at

expresses the present (the rose garden) which has already
lapsed into the past. The image with its Donnean overlay
is somewhat complex. The unseen eyebeam—if we follow
the Donne parallel—resembles the single vision of lovers
who in the rose garden are "one another's best." But since
the unseen eyebeam is here singular (in Donne it is
plural) and since it is *seen*, and the roses (the lovers and
all such lovers) have the look of flowers that are looked
at, I infer that this is an elaborate way of indicating that
self-consciousness has already terminated the lover's at-
oneness,[42] that this "self" consciousness as a matter of
fact partially implies a feeling of being surveyed by what
in the *Family Reunion* is called "the self which persisted
only as an eye, seeing." This eye, in *Family Reunion*, is
later identified with the judging eye of God. But whatever
warning the eyebeam conveys, the action which the bird
instigates, follows. It is made feasible by a new relation
with "them": "There they were as our guests, accepted
and accepting" (line 32). The word "guests" seems peculiar. If we are reading literally and take "them" to be

Adam and Eve, it does seem somewhat odd to call our first parents "guests." But if we accept the idea that we are re-enacting something that might have occurred a long time ago between Us no. 2 and "them," then this language perhaps indicates a leap in erotic sophistication. "They" become an adult mode of action that We no. 2 here entertained, and our new mode of action was by them taken for granted. As a result, in the next line, our conjunction with them is enacted: they and we move together in time to the unheard music hidden in the shrubbery. These images convey the sense of plenitude that follows each conjunction. But the plentitude is followed by new emptiness. Lines 32–33 convey the sense of conjunction and plenitude:

> *There they were as our guests, accepted and accepting*
> *So we moved, and they, in a formal pattern.*

But the fullness is followed once more (lines 33–36) by imagery suggesting emptiness:

> *So we moved, and they, in a formal pattern,*
> *Along the empty alley, into the box circle,*
> *To look down into the drained pool.*
> *Dry the pool, dry concrete, brown edged.*

If we read the journey into the garden as a symbolic account of phases of love, the images of the formal pattern, the empty alley, and the box circle are perhaps descriptive of the type of consciousness which Eliot mentioned in connection with the balcony scene in *Romeo and Juliet* where, he said, Shakespeare shows his lovers melting into unconsciousness of their isolated selves, shows the human soul in the process of forgetting itself.[43] The box circle would contrast with the rose garden, where the roses have the look of flowers that are looked at; the "formal pattern" whereby the box circle and the drained pool are reached is that which all natural desire takes (the boarhound and the boar follow it); the alley is empty of flowers, and the ecstasy of the center is what in "Marina" is called "the ecstasy of the animals, meaning/ Death." The drained pool is that death.

We might notice that the "end" of which the bird's second call was the beginning, is to look down into the drained pool. The wording is such as to emphasize the fact that what we and "they" move *for* is "to look down into the drained pool," which seems a puzzling goal for such splendid arrangements. Yet this same paradox appears in "Marina":

> *Those who sharpen the tooth of the dog, meaning*
> *Death*
> *Those who glitter with the glory of humming-*
> *bird, meaning*
> *Death*
> *Those who sit in the stye of contentment, meaning*
> *Death*
> *Those who suffer the ecstasy of animals, meaning*
> *Death.*

In addition, we may wonder why both "they" and we are united not only in the desire to adhere to the formal pattern but united also in the desire to "look down into the drained pool," an end which seems somewhat perverse for "them" if not for us, for "them," that is, who have known the splendor of the rose garden. The explanation, perhaps, is that "they" cannot stay still in the rose garden, as we cannot stay still in the box circle, that both "they" and we because of our estrangement are driven by the need for self-extinction. That is why we both come expectantly to the drained pool. We thus have a double conjunction of us and "them," a conjunction in life and death as it were—the aim of the aestheticism of them and the Laurentian naturalism of us is self extinction. The cult of nature becomes the cult of death as Eliot once remarked.[44]

Nevertheless, it is impossible to disguise the astonishing fact of the third center in the garden. At the heart of the garden of Adonis is a dry pool, dry concrete, brown edged. This "bowl" resembles the bowl of rose leaves with which Scene 1 ended. Only this is the end of a corridor for which there is no natural exit by following the deception of the thrush. The thrush is silent. Imagination is useless.

We may be puzzled as to logic of the miracle that enters at this point. If I understand the significance of our following "them," we have been re-enacting two ways that lead to death: the upward way of "them" and the downward way of Us no. 2. Both were sinful. Yet, despite this, the equivalent of the Holy Spirit descends, the equivalent of the Incarnation rises slowly, and there is the revelatory emblem of the Ultimate Reality. Are we supposed to see some causal connection between the magical strategies and the transcendent revelation?

Eliot is evidently carefully threading difficult theological concerns. If I follow the pattern, it indicates that his vision here and now indicates that all three intentions, "theirs" originally, "ours" secondarily (We no. 2), and our present one (We no. 1), are intentions to re-establish contact with Ultimate Reality from which we are estranged. These intentions, however flawed, were not, are not, and will not be without their fulfillment, though that fulfillment has to be by birth and rebirth into new suffering. In short, out of their involvement, We no. 2 were born; and out of "our" intercourse, "you and I" (We no. 1) were born.

A feature of Eliot's syntax in this scene is the way he uses "and" to signal intersection of a transcendent element with the dramatic progression. "And the bird called." "And the unseen eyebeam crossed . . ." "And the pool was filled." "And the lotus." It is as if he uses *and* in order to suggest that whatever the connection with the dramatic action, it is not causal. The omission of the "and" in line 39 where the still point is revealed, is perhaps to suggest that what is always present is not subject to relativity of any kind.

No commentary, I imagine, is needed to explain the symbolism of the three lines (37–39) that constitute the climax of the upward way.

> And the pool was filled with water out of sunlight,
> And the lotus rose, quietly, quietly,
> The surface glittered out of heart of light.

The first line images the event that *Ash-Wednesday* celebrates: the appearance of a new life in the midst of death.

The second line symbolizes the response that the poet was unable to make in *Ash-Wednesday,* the response of life lived without attention to the profit and loss of the man. If we are looking before and afterward, the lotus is a plant that contrasts with rose and boxwood. If we are watching movements, the descent of sunlight is a new exemplification of the way down, the lotus of the way up. But the final line images the mystery of Divine Love that is at once the upward and downward way, symbolized by glitter. We shall appreciate this line better if we ask what ultimate insight into spiritual life would be missing were we left only with the descent of sunlight and ascent of lotus. What would be missing is the intuition which in theology is expressed by the statement that in God essence and existence are synonymous, or that being takes nonbeing into itself. The point is not without importance because in this glitter image the meaning as it were of *their* ecstasy and *our* despair is re-expressed.

This at any rate suggests an interpretation for the third appearance of "them": "And they were behind us, reflected in the pool" (line 40). "They" are what we intended to find in the beginning. As it turned out, it was not "them" but that of which they were but images or echoes that we intended. But here the intention is finally fulfilled. How should we interpret their final appearance? If we take their appearance in terms of what follows, it is their appearance that terminates the beatific vision, just as in the *Family Reunion* "they" do. "They" in short are our curse, the curse of what the Buddhists call "individuality." No wonder the cloud of "flesh" (the principle of individuation) intervenes between the sun and the pool. But if we look at the "image" another way, if we visualize the line, "And they were behind us, reflected in the pool," it gives a final image of conjunction: "they" and we, conjoined in the ultimate life. If I see this image rightly, "they" and "we" are transfigured: we become, not what we have been. We fuse to become the image of the way up and the way down, the *path* to the ultimate reality. Thus one might reason that the image is prophetic. "They" as *they* are behind us. But "they" in the pool are also before us. And the way toward them is through us (We no. 1), the estranged ones, the corridored selves. The rest of the poem is the working out of *our* destiny.

Nevertheless, the image of the "them" and us reflected in the pool undoubtedly sets off the beginning of the expulsion. Another way to see the logic of this is to say that our confrontation at this moment with "them" makes us realize that this ecstasy, however ecstatic, is dream, not fact. We, like Celia, in *The Cocktail Party*, feel that the dream is not enough.[45] We reach out to flesh. Thus we repeat the *hamartia* of the children in the garden. Yet our doing so now has a different context from theirs. It is a hopeful sign, as in Auden's *The Sea and the Mirror*, Prospero's adieu to Ariel marks the beginning of real spiritual life.

I am not sure how many ways we ought to interpret the return of the thrush (lines 42–45):

> Go, *said the bird, for the leaves were full of children,*
> *Hidden excitedly, containing laughter.*
> Go, go, go, *said the bird: human kind*
> *Cannot bear very much reality.*

What he speaks is in the past tense; what we hear is what we heard long ago; I am not sure that it has the same meaning now as it had then. I am inclined to think that our submitting to the deception of the thrush indicates our willingness to take up "our" reality. It seems significant that the thrush as such does not reappear in the poem; and that when at the end of the poem we have rejoined the children, it is not under his auspices that we do so.

If we think of the concluding lines as spoken by the poet in the present tense, we must think of him as occupying a new, a third position. He has got his history centered. He is on the way to accepting his destiny. This is the happening that makes Scenes 1 and 2 an act. The poet has been given the ideal of his freedom, not quite the freedom he had intended when he started for Burnt Norton, but freedom which comes from understanding necessity and accepting it.

iv

Eliot has clearly divided the movement of Section II into three stanzas, then with a half verse, marked the place in the third stanza where a coda begins. If we look at these stanzas, and at the coda, we can tell just from their appearance on the page that the poet is doing something quite different here from what he did in Section I. What? The best answer is that he *sings* and *dances*. Section II is like a choric interlude; the protagonist is the chorus; and we must not think of the interlude as a pause in the struggle but as the poet's exertions to bring the next phase to successful conclusion.

What is the poet trying to do? We might look at the very last line in the section, "Only through time time is conquered," and say that he is trying to reach that line. This, however, would be a cryptic statement of what he must attain to. What must he do? He must take the first step toward accepting his destiny. Think of the poet standing outside the garden, perhaps in the corridor, which is the symbol of his destiny in its unfavorable aspect, the symbol, that is, of time or existence as an imprisonment. What he must do is accept the corridor, the unacceptable. The last line in Section I indicates that he has taken the first step in doing so. He has justified time, which we must not think of as something abstract, but as something as concrete as the poet's feet rising and falling in the corridor. In justifying time, he has justified himself, and reconciled himself (intellectually) to himself. If we recollect the degree of alienation that was expressed by the broken verse in Section I, we should be prepared to see the broken verse at the end of Section II as a return of the self to itself, but a return that is reconciled.

We cannot interpret the movements in Section II without looking at them as stages in a progression, unfolding phases of an intention; but at the same time we need to remember what these steps are moving from. Section II is a "between-nessing" in that behind the poet is Burnt Norton, the garden, the revelatory experiencing of "them" behind us reflected in the pool. In front of him is the place of disaffection, the time-ridden world of Section III. Section II is a bridging, a prolongation and a preparation. Only by thinking of what the poet is moving from and toward can we appreciate the internal and external reasons for the *form* in which he acts. He *sings*, because with part of himself he is still outside of himself, and only in song should he speak of the mysteries that have been revealed. He is compelled to bear witness, nevertheless, like the chorus in *Murder in the Cathedral*, in order to testify to the meaning of what has been given. At the same time, he is back inside himself, inside his "sole self," his body. His dancing represents an ideal bodily act; it is what his body might do. This choric interlude has for me the quality of transport and artificiality. The transport is expressed by the song; the artificiality by the dance. The poet's dancing is perhaps a bit of an oddity even to him (as it must certainly be to the aunts and uncles in *The Family Reunion*); but it is as if the music takes possession of his body; he moves and he moves not; the dance moves through him; he suffers it a little awkwardly; but his saying yes to the awkwardness of the dance is a hopeful sign. This is the way to reconciliation with the corridor.

Once we make what the poet is doing the point of attention we begin to attend in the right way to what he is saying. For example, each stanza represents an act of assimilation; each is an act of saying *yes*. If we look ahead to Section V, we will see that the poet there gives names to three categories of being. There is (1) that which is only moving, words or music, feet, or selves; there is (2) the form, the pattern whereby that which otherwise is only moving reaches the stillness; and finally there is (3) the stillness which is the still point, that which is the real reality. At the start of the poem, these three features of existence are separated from one another. The feet reject the corridor, and the corridor runs in an opposite direction from garden and still point. At the end the categories are in a state of equilibrized tension. But here in

Section II the poet is saying "yes" (Stanza 1) first to the form, the pattern, second to the still point, and third to that which is only moving—the up-down self. He is saying this "yes" artificially, in the form of an ideal act, in a poem in short; but the ideal act is preparatory to the same act in Section V.

The first stanza, the most obviously lyrical, sings the way to the still point, it sings "the dance," or, if we like, it sings "the wheel of existence," or from another point of view, it sings the Heraclitian *logos*, the way that is simultaneously up and down. This is a very important "beginning," for at a stroke the poet takes possession of the corridor. What strikes me as interesting is the way the song echoes the protagonist's ambivalent feelings about the process: words like garlic, mud, blood, scars, artery, lymph, sodden floor are echoes of a repulsion. The struggle is the struggle to suffer the dance's power to assimilate the life of the body.

Some of the difficulties of this stanza seem to me to cease to be difficulties once we know where to plant our feet. Though it sounds like nonsense, I wonder if our standpoint is not the sun? We are making a tree-of-life figure, and according to one tradition, this tree has its roots in the air.[46] When the poet begins (lines 49–50)

> Garlic and sapphires in the mud
> Clot the bedded axle-tree

has he not bedded his consciousness in the mud as it were? Garlic and sapphires are olfactory and tactile images of dis-ease. Sight can make nothing of these images because we have no eyes until we reach line ten. But the effect of being head down in mud is agitation. The agitation proceeds in a rhythm of ascent. The first sentence, for example, consists of two lines, and the pulse is like that we hear consciously at the end: the pattern on the sodden floor. This is the head's intuition of root being. The second sentence consists of three lines and the effect is as if we are mounting a trunk. It is hard to tell whether the "trilling wire" is or is not an auditory image. It is *touch* on the verge of sound. The third sentence stretches across ten lines and the motion is intricate and diverse; the sentence consists of two statements, the first ending with "tree" in line 57, the second beginning with "we," but the poet places no period between the two for reasons which would be interesting to explore. Perhaps he means us to see that this is a break which is no break. In the first statement, we are inside the trunk still; the "drift of stars" is not something we see; it is something felt the way we feel the guided movement of a boat. It is what is inside us (lymph) felt as if it were outside us, and it is felt that way because blood and lymph are in the process of climbing to "summer in the tree" where leaves stand to the light like stars. From the word "garlic" to the word "tree," we follow a steadily upward track that is "eyeless"; this is the hidden music of the shrubbery of Section I. But having reached leaves and light, "we"—with all the connotations of Section I—appear, and we are moving in the reverse direction, downward with sight onto the leaf, and downward with our ears to the sound on the sodden floor where the boarhound and the boar perform their rites. It may seem strange that what is blind, struggles upward and what sees, "falls." But the poet is perhaps merely repeating again the pattern of "they" and "we" in the garden. But he now makes the third significant movement that is paradoxical and reconciling; "we" keep right on going, right past the sodden floor and the animals to the stars. How? Simply by virtue of the fact that our feet are on the sun; we are not seeing this so much as enacting it, and at this point, our downward way passes the earth and goes right on up to the stars, beyond our earth, that are illuminated by the sun where our feet are planted.

What is the poet protagonist doing in this stanza? He is singing the life of the axletree in such a way as, by the end of the stanza, to be the axletree, reconciling "the trill" and the wire, that which is only moving and the way. How does he do this? By inverting himself, putting his feet where his head has been, putting his head where his feet have been. But if we need a formula—in Stanza 1, he is *suffering* the dance of life, he is dancing the wheel of existence.

In the action in Stanza 1, the first of three dances, the poet combines the "detail" and the "pattern"; he does so by ceasing to try to turn the wheel himself, by letting go and suffering the vibrations to follow the revolutions of the wheel toward reconciliation. We notice that the wheel rolls him up, then down, then into the paradoxical down-up that is the third way that the poet is moving toward. In the language of *Murder in the Cathedral*, the poet in Stanza 1 is fixing himself

In an eternal action, an eternal patience
To which all must consent that it may be willed
And which all must suffer that they may will it,
That the pattern may subsist, for the pattern is the action
And the suffering, that the wheel may turn and still
Be forever still.[47]

In Stanza 2, as soon as he announces "At the still point of the turning world," we know that the poet his moved into the next phase of the reconciliation, the dance whereby he centers the finite center in the infinite one. The first stanza seems more song than dance; it is about "the dance along the artery"; but the second stanza seems more dance than song; the poet we might say reverses his position, puts his feet on the earth again, but with his feet imitating the light which glittered out of heart of light in the fountain. His head now is toward the sun. Anyone who has attempted to memorize this stanza may have noted how hard it is to keep in mind. It is as if it consists of distinct details that appear just at the point of self-extinction, and of a clear-cut pattern that emerges only to efface itself. The poet-protagonist is like a ballerina concentrating on motionless motion achieved by suspending herself on the vibrations of her toes, breaking the figure from moment to moment only to show the difference between actual immobility and this and actual linear movement and this.

The effort consists of the difficulty of expressing the

inexpressible without faltering. The feet are drawn as it were to do what the head would condemn: the cloud speaking of the sun. Even as the attempt is made, the wheel rotates, the ballerina gradually fades toward the circumference; the language drifts from "At the still point." "At the still point" "There is only the dance" to the thrice repeated "I" of "I can only say," "I can say," "I cannot say."

Against the spiralling movement from center to orbit, the poet repeatedly centers the Center by uncentering specious centers, the false center of the self-centered, the false center of the order of mere order, or mere pattern. The stylistic feature of this stanza is the recurrence of the negative conjunction "neither" which echoes perhaps the "Neti . . . Neti" of the Hindu mystic. But what we need to note is that this negative conjunction occurs in "the middle of the way," in the middle stanza, not at the end. This is not the still point, this is the poet at the still point, which is to say, this is the poet enacting what the poet was seeing in Section I. What we notice about the poet's negative conjunctions is that they are *conjunctions*; they are negative between-nessings that are not so much obliterative as purgational and restorative. They restore the dancer and the dance by relating them to their fulfillment. The second stanza in short is the second step in the poet's reconciliation with what had hitherto seemed ruin. It is living out of the truth of the third way, the negative way that he will take in fact in Sections III, IV, and V.

We gather the purgative and restorative effects of this dance best when we constantly relate what the poet does to the states of mind he is just emerging from (lines 64–66):

At the still point of the turning world. Neither flesh nor
  fleshless;
Neither from nor towards; at the still point, there the dance
  is,
But neither arrest nor movement.

"At the still point of the turning world" is a cry of discovery by one who has just glimpsed from the maze, where all corridors seem to lead to corridors, a third reality which transforms corridors and their echoing footfalls into something other. In "Neither flesh nor fleshless," the *neither* is the cry of a person who is "doing a new thing" and that new thing signals release from intolerable alternatives of rose garden or drained pool; in "Neither from nor towards," the *neither* is the signal of release from the boarhound and the boar, the flight from what has been, the flight toward what might have been. And the release is not a release into nothingness but into the plenitude of a real present: "At the still point, *there* the dance is." This is the cry of life found, that what has been craved has being; moreover the *there* liberates the dance from space. The dance along the artery is not *in* the artery but in the still point, the next *neither* makes the point even more clearly: "But neither arrest nor movement." This *neither* releases the feet from the impulse to freeze the dance (as Keats seems tempted to do in the Grecian Urn, or as Amy does in *The Family Reunion*) or from the impulse (such as Harry Monchensey's wife illustrates) to destroy the fixed order that controls the crying shadow. I am tempted to say that we have here the most satisfying sequence of negations in the English language. The poet reverses the behaviour complained of in *Ash-Wednesday*. Here he denies before the world and affirms between the rocks (lines 66–68):

> And do not call it fixity,
> Where past and future are gathered. Neither movement
> from nor towards,
> Neither ascent nor decline.

The command "Do not call it fixity" is a warning cry that might seem unnecessary unless we think of it as like the dancer's exclamation, a warning to himself against a mistake that might easily be made. Taken as cry, it tells us that the dancer is still centering the Center. But taken as command, it perhaps tells us that the dancer is centering the Center from farther out; consciousness has been widened; the dancer is at the point where he might see himself spinning like a planet, and might see eternity as idea rather than as act, eternity, that is, as infinite time. It was this false eternity that constituted the hell in which the poem began. To liberate the center from the suggestion of fixation, the poet makes it not a place but a realization: "where past and future are *gathered*." Past and future are "gathered" in the sense that their "meaning" is gained: *This* is what pastness meant; this is what futurity meant; this is what the sense of the past made us sensible of through regret, and what the sense of the future made us sensible of through yearning. When the poet says: "Neither movement from nor towards," he appears to be repeating the second line of the stanza: "Neither from nor towards"; but insertion of the word *movement* changes the coloration, makes the center the place of vibrant realization.

When the poet says (lines 68–69),

> *Except for the point, the still point,*
> *There would be no dance, and there is only the dance.*

I get the sense of the dancer's beginning to run down. There is a suggestion of a contrast between what the dancer has been doing and what that doing has been mimicking. "There is only the dance" releases the man from dancing forever just here; it focuses the real dance; makes the dancer's dance but a manifestation of *the* dance; *the* dance is like the joy of the Creator without which the ecstasy of the creature would not be joy but madness.

When in the last two lines of the stanza, the poet re-intrudes the personal pronoun, he is dancing again in his own circle, and the still point is where we *have been:*

> *I can only say, there we have been: but I cannot say where.*
> *And I cannot say, how long, for that is to place it in time.*

Though back in his personal center, the point seems to be that he can step over the forms of space and time without tripping. We are apt, however, to be most struck

by the claim that is made for us: "*there* we have been."
We have never opened the door into the rose garden, yet
we have been at the still point. This perhaps means that
even in the corridor we were *there*.

If the theme of the first stanza is "wheeling," and the
theme of the second is "centering," the theme of the
third is "staying still." The remarkable thing about the
second dance is the way the centered center takes into itself the movement of the vibrating dancer; the remarkable thing about the third is the way the restless dancer
is embraced by the stillness of the center. Nouns dominate this stanza as negative conjunctions dominated the
second. The first effect is to divest the self of its own
spinning movement by merging it in a state of stillness
spreading from center to circumference like a radiance in
which a spinning planet does not so much spin as breathe.
The poet in the first few lines does something like let a
bird out of a cage: "The inner freedom. . . . The release . . . release. . . ." What he is released from continues to vibrate with the trilling rhythm (three unstressed
syllables) that is the signature of the finite self raising and
lowering its winged feet in the corridor (lines 72–74):

The inner freedom from the practical desire,
The release from action and suffering, release from the inner
And the outer compulsion.

The release from the finite is a release that keeps it alive,
and that reconciles it to itself. The climactic reconciliation is made manifest by the poet's reversal of attitude
toward the flesh, and mankind (lines 81–84):

> Yet the enchainment of past and future
> Woven in the weakness of the changing body,
> Protects mankind from heaven and damnation
> Which flesh cannot endure.

He had used the word *release* earlier to signal the shift
into the world of the flicker. Here the selfhood of the
self is accepted because the axis on which it spins has
been coincident with the Axis Mundi.

In these four lines, the poet's vocabulary reflects the shift back to the quotidian from the world of light. Words like "enchainment," "weakness," "damnation," express the poet's reaction to his re-entry into the cage of the flesh. Yet his language should be contrasted with that of the thrush. That representative of the aesthetic life is scornful. This somewhat differently inspired voice is compassionate. The reason why human kind cannot bear very much reality is suggested. Like the Chorus in *Murder in the Cathedral*, the self chooses the flicker because of the danger of the alternatives.

The second act of *Burnt Norton* ends here really, but not actually. The poet inside the corridor repeats in prosaic terms the reconciliation achieved in the dance. He conceptualizes what he saw gathered at the still point. When he finally says (line 91), "Only through time time is conquered," he is epitomizing the realization that only by experiencing the pointlessness of time can we experience what it points to. This line therefore could be taken as the termination of Act I and II. The flight to Burnt Norton had been an incomplete strategy for conquering time. But the strategy had prepared for the proper one— the way down—now to follow.

v

In *Burnt Norton* III, the dramatic action seems easy to perceive. "Here is a place of disaffection," the poet says in the first line, like an actor calling attention to the scene where he is placed. He proceeds to characterize the place rather exhaustively. Having done so, he takes action. "Descend lower," he commands, "descend only/ Into the world of perpetual solitude."

The connections between Section III and the preceding ones seem also easy to see. If Section I, the visit to Burnt Norton, is a vacation, Section III is a return to the urban prison. Both sections confront time's corridor, and record the poet's response to its intolerability. If the visionary trip into the rose garden is the way up (away from time) to the real reality, the descent into the world not world is what the epigraph assures us is the "same way." In both, what is important is that the poet takes stock of an intolerable situation and acts. We can see that at Burnt Norton, what the poet reacts to is essentially his own private predicament, whereas in London he confronts "some huge disaster,/ Some monstrous mistake and aberration/ Of all men, of the world," [48] which he cannot put in order. We may also see that the "action" in entering the rose garden is not really the poet's "act"; it is a grace which happens to him. But the descent is his, a decision *he* must make. We may notice finally that this action which he undertakes freely at the end of Section III completes the action commanded by the bird ("Go, go, go . . .") at the end of Section I.

We see clearly enough that the action here taken is important in the pattern of the work as a whole. The poet-protagonist here commits himself to *his* world (to his personal, rather than cosmic destiny), not in an ideal choric dance as in Section II, but actually, by involving himself in business at the heart of London where he works. The admonition to descend lower is equivalent to Harry's decision to pursue the specters rather than have them pursue him; and Harry's course meant "A care over the lives of humble people. The lesson of ignorance, of incurable diseases." Here the poet's course is less specific.

The dramatic framework of Eliot's third act is thus quite clear. What is not clear, however, is the filling of the framework. I find I do not at first understand what the style is doing, partly because what it seems to be doing seems to be irrelevant to the action. If I study the way the poet treats the "place of disaffection," his treatment seems to be characterized by something like tumidity: "Eructation of unhealthy souls," for example, seems an expression of a contempt in excess of the facts as they appear. Contempt for the "other man"—but not for one's self—is a state of mind that we meet with in Eliot's prose, but less frequently in his poetry. So when I seem to find it here, it suggests a kind of Pharasaical thank-God-I-am-not-as-other-men-are, the effect of which is to compromise the descent into darkness. The poet seems to be doing the right thing for the wrong reason.

John Betjeman has written an appreciative comment on the way Section III of *Burnt Norton* expresses Eliot's sensitivity to the poetry of urban London.[49] I see what Mr. Betjeman is responding to; it is in the poem at this point; but is it relevant to the "action" that the poet-as-protagonist is taking? The London place names evoke memories of Eliot's condemnation of Milton's use of place names in *Paradise Lost*,[50] and we question whether Eliot is indulging *his* sensibility, or projecting what moves the mind of his poet-protagonist.

Yet this seems so far from Eliot's usual practice that I should like to examine the situation once again. Could we say that there are two points of crisis in *Burnt Norton?* The first is when he stands in the corridors of Burnt Norton and confronts the fact that the vacation has provided no exit from his prison. The second is when he stands in the Gloucester Road Station. What is the danger here?

In trying to answer this question, I find I raise several others. Why does the poet's technique labor so hard? Is the function of the laboring style but to discredit the place of disaffection? Is the temptation of the place so insidious as to require a surcharge of contempt? But this line of questioning leads nowhere; a poet who begins by glorifying daylight and night has obviously rejected twilight. We come back to the original question: What is the danger that the laboring style struggles to dispel?

When I re-examine Eliot's manner in this section I seem to note that he is like one repeating a charm. He seems to circle everything, if he can, three times—compelled, as it were, to keep the basic aspects closed in (lines 92–94, 94–97, 98–100):

> *Here is a place of disaffection* [once]
> *Time before and time after* [twice]
> *In a dim light* [thrice].
>
> > *neither daylight*
> *Investing form with lucid stillness* [once]

Turning shadow into transient beauty [twice]
With slow rotation suggesting permanence [thrice]

Nor darkness to purify the soul [once]
Emptying the sensual with deprivation [twice]
Cleansing affection from the temporal. [thrice]

But when the poet contemplates life under the flicker, a struggle develops between the poet trying to keep his measures, and the chaos of the place he enters. The poet gradually loses his feet; as the imagery grows rougher and windier, he seems in danger of being whirled out over the landscape. The poet's "not here, not here the darkness in this twittering world" is as if he were blown away in a cloud of bats.

Could it be that the insidious danger here is, not that the poet will be tempted back into the world, but that unless he takes immediate and decisive action, that world will overwhelm him? Could we emphasize that the peculiar horror of this world is that it holds all the cards as it were, and without being anything, can transform whatever comes near it into its own characterlessness? Nonparticipation in this world is participation; even contemplation of it, the effort to comprehend is involvement. Thus comments on the poet's tone, or attitude, are irrelevant. These are not people. This is not a moral world. This is a place of disaffection. And whoever comes to it must come, like Odysseus to the land of the dead, *instructed*.

With the descent, the poet starts counting again, invoking what he seeks nine times. The large words he uses are abstract nouns that contrast with the present participles he had used at the outset. It is as if the motions he invokes at this point are but ideas in his head. But before the end, the compulsive spell-casting stops and suddenly the "way" as it were lights up. The last line of the section signals that the poet is "safe." Why? At the outset he was in the place of disaffection, and time there was "time *before* and time *after*"—which is to say, states of anxiety. Now "time past" and "time future" are the "metalled ways" of a world behind him.

vi

Section IV of *Burnt Norton* is so entirely pure lyric or pure vision that nothing seems to remain for commentary to do. Yet Section IV is part of a progression. Guardedly, then, we may ask: What is it we admire in this lyric? Then, what does the lyric mean? These two questions turn out to be inseparable, and as soon as we raise the second, almost every detail provokes curiosity. When we have given whatever answers we are capable of, the lyric remains lyrical as before.

The special quality of Section IV is immediacy. Like some of Shakespeare's songs, the words seem to come straight out of the emotion without premeditation, uninfluenced by the existence of other lyrics in the world. The fact that Eliot's opening line echoes a fifteenth-century lyric [51] does not alter the matter. The effect of Section IV is that of lyrical purity, and this effect is what matters. If we compare this song with that beginning Section II (Garlic and sapphires in the mud), *that* song is a song-convention; the alienated singer there consciously participates in a choric outcry. He is both inside and outside the moment. But here, the protagonist is wholly within his emotion. It is real, not ideal.

If we contemplate Section IV as a part of a total action, we may come around to the opinion that our appreciation is not merely aesthetic. What the poet has done is write truthfully of what is beautiful. The aesthetic pleasure is due to our sense of the poet's having recovered his voice, a beautiful event. For the purity of outcry is somehow connected with the "death" that ended the struggle in Section III. This lyric is like a bird crying out before daylight. The bird is frightened. But his fright is a sign that he is still alive.

Having identified the beauty of the song with its truth, we may with less offense, perhaps, consider what some of the details may mean. First, where is it that the poet-protagonist sings from? He sings from "the world of perpetual solitude/ World not world." that he descended into at the end of Section III. Thus the "black cloud" that has *buried* the day, contrasts with the cloud that "passed" in Section I. *That* cloud produced the twilight world of Section III. But this one produces the "darkness." Perhaps the difference is like the distinction Kierkegaard draws between being in despair (as all men, he says, are) without knowing it and being on the other side of despair. Or perhaps it is like the difference between one's own shadow striding to meet one and the shadow of the red rock—which Teresias invites the protagonist to enter in *The Waste Land*. (This "shadow" brings relief.)

Second, why, from the "grave," does the protagonist ask just the questions that he does? What do his questions imply about his state of mind? If we attempt to answer in the context of the whole poem, we may come to the conclusion that though his questions are good and bad, the questioner has reached a place where all that he does may turn to good. For example, what the poet asks for is, in a sense, prayed for. His questions are an involuntary prayer for continued being. This is good. For one who has been at the still point (Section I), and has celebrated the possibilities of existence (Section II), not to make inquiry would be a symptom of indifference. The questions are a sign of love. On the other hand, the form of the prayer is ambiguous. To turn from the world not world to the garden is to gardenize that which is not garden (and to disobey the injunction of St. John of the Cross to avoid "images" in the dark night of the soul). We seem to see this more clearly when the answer to the poet's queries comes (lines 136–38):

> After the kingfisher's wing
> Has answered light to light, and is silent, the light is still
> At the still point of the turning world.

It is as if the poet has reached such a state of susceptibility that merely to raise the questions is to detect the impurity of motive behind them. The lyric ends therefore in the state of faith symbolized by acceptance of the darkness.

vii

Speaking of his friend, Lionel Johnson, William Butler Yeats once declared that "all his Greek and Latin learning seemed/ A long blast upon the horn that brought/ A little nearer to his thought/ A measureless consummation that he dreamed." [52] Section V of *Burnt Norton* is pervaded by the sound of such a horn. There is no ambiguity (fair is foul and foul is fair) such as pervades Section I; no equivocation such as in Section II causes the poet to give himself only in the artifice of art; no mixture of contempt and helplessness as in III, or sound of wavering as in IV. If, as Aristotle says, life is action and the end of life is an action, we here have the poet re-assuming his station and duties as an artist. Yet it would be wrong to assume that the action of Section V is free from struggle.

To characterize this struggle we need to look at what the poet is preoccupied with in the two stanzas that constitute Section V. *Words* are the dominant concern in Stanza 1: (Words move. . . . Words reach. . . . Words strain. . . .) *Movement* or *motion* seems to be the concern of Stanza 2. And the poet's effort in the first stanza is to state how to make words move right, to make them be still and still moving; in the second stanza his effort is to say how movement must transcend movement, how the moving must still be still. Though this pattern sounds artificial, it is not: the poet here begins the practice of his art on a new basis. Such a practice is not free of peril. His procedure, like that, therefore, of the spiritual proficients for whom St. John of the Cross writes *The Ascent of Mt. Carmel,* must be a conscious exercise. When the poet, in Section III, makes his descent into darkness, that is like Kierkegaard's movement of infinite resignation. But the next movement that he makes, in Section V, is like that of Kierkegaard's Knight of Faith. It is the taking back of everything that had been given up, and this, as Kierkegaard states, is an act far harder than the first.[53] When the poet sits still, he is in danger of staying still, i.e. making *his* stillness his end; and when he strives to be still and still moving (to reassume, like Peter Quilpe, his metier even after the bottom has dropped out of everything),[54] he runs the risk of making formal movement his end. He is between the horns of the dilemma that gored him fatally in *Ash-Wednesday*. He has to exert his will to re-linquish his will. This is why he struggles in Stanza 1 to meditate on the way words must be still and still moving, and in Stanza 2 on the way movement must be moving and still still.

A distinctive feature of the struggle that composes Section V is that the place of the struggle has been clarified. The contest is now restricted to the world of air, where the issue can be decided by right thinking, which is to say by proper use of words. What I mean is similar, I be-lieve, to what Josiah Royce means when he says that man's moral freedom is constituted by the power of attention.[55] We can be possessed by the truth if we are sufficiently at-tentive. The word of being is common, and the truth will liberate us. Our imprisonment is due to inattentiveness. Words are, therefore, our means of putting ourselves in position to be grasped by the truth. What Eliot is doing is committing himself to the life of words.

His effort in Stanza 1 passes through two phases. First he is concerned to penetrate what words *do*; then what words *suffer*. In the first phase the poet wrestles with words and produces (in my judgment) some of the most tortured English in the poem. The language at first is de-ceptively simple (lines 139–41):

> *Words move, music moves*
> *Only in time; but that which is only living*
> *Can only die.*

The thrice repeated "only" becomes a troubled intima-tion that the poet is concerned about something more than the obvious truism that words and music move in time. Something about the fate of words is here echoing the fate of man. The boarhound and the boar move *in* time too, but they do not move *only* in time. Men and

words, however, *move only* in time. The boarhound and
the boar are not free; they are moved, and therefore they
participate in eternity, reconciled among the stars. But
words are free and they move, not in space, but only in
time, in the place of disaffection, in the human sphere. To
have the unique potentiality of "only living" is to have the
potentiality of "only dying." Unlike other creatures, words
can live to themselves (be shapes without form) and die
to themselves (become like the ghosts that enter Limbo,
rejected by God and the Devil). Such at any rate seems
to be the profounder meaning signalled by the poet's
repetition of the word "reach" and his play on the difference between "silence" and "stillness" (lines 141–44):

> *Words, after speech, reach*
> *Into the silence. Only by the form, the pattern,*
> *Can words or music reach*
> *The stillness. . . .*

The *silence* is death, darkness, nonbeing. The words reach,
but nothing answers: there is silence in heaven. The stillness, on the other hand, is life, light, Being: the still point.
The poet enforces this distinction on himself because having descended into the "world, not world" he has with his
words, "reached into the silence" but has not "reached the
stillness." The poet in these few lines has dramatized the
necessity under which he labors to state how the impossible may yet be.

It is at this point that I seem to notice the language
showing signs of strain. The analogy of the Chinese jar—
so beautiful and appropriate to the comparison that we
think the poet is making: that between patterned speech
and a Chinese vase—twists in the middle and something
syntactically rough and difficult emerges: "By the form,
words *can* reach the stillness as a Chinese jar still moves
perpetually in its stillness." The mind protests the confusion of possible with actual, means with end. But the
justification is that precisely this is what the protagonist
must do. He must show the miracle, not as possible, but
as accomplished. The illogic is the illogic of starting to tell

the truth about a temporal act by a space analogy; the spatial picture falsifies the act; he corrects the falsification by forcing *us* to become the Chinese jar we contemplate. He translates the spatial form into temporal terms.

The struggle to state how to be still and still moving leads to another comparison that language must reach for. The stillness of the Chinese jar is succeeded by the "stillness" of the violin (lines 146–48):

> Not the stillness of the violin, while the note lasts,
> Not that only, but the co-existence,
> Or say that the end precedes the beginning.

In the space of five lines we have "the silence," "the stillness," "its stillness," "the stillness of the violin." If the *silence* is "non-being," and *"the stillness"* is being, then "its stillness" is the pattern whereby the Chinese jar becomes an incarnation of "the stillness." The violin's stillness becomes like the stillness of the earth in the jar, or like the individual word in the sentence. The violin becomes a symbol of the poet himself, and the point he is here enforcing on himself is again that it is not enough for him to be still as the violin is still. He must be still and still moving as the vase is. But just when we have reached the violin's stillness and separated it from the vase's, the poet scrambles the syntax again with "not that only," a phrase which, logically, so qualifies the preceding line as almost to cancel it. He then launches into a furious effort to make good the contradiction (lines 146–51):

> Not the stillness of the violin, while the note lasts,
> Not that only, but the co-existence,
> Or say that the end precedes the beginning,
> And the end and the beginning were always there
> Before the beginning and after the end.
> And all is always now.

What strikes me here is the struggle to speak true even in the face of contradiction, and the struggle in addition, to have concentration without elimination. "Not the stillness of the violin" corrects the tendency of the instrument to identify *its* end (the stillness of the violin) with its *end* (the sounding of the note). "Not that only," however, corrects the tendency of the pattern, the form to identify its stillness with *the* stillness (the still point), at the expense of the violin-like self whose "end" is the still point, not the form; so that in the light of what is *in* the violin potentially, the form is but the means whereby the instrument reached the end. It is to sound the mutuality of violin and sounding note that the poet uses the word "co-existence" and then glosses it with three lines in which "end" and "beginning" oscillate between the temporal and the eternal and we see the poet achieving, consciously, in his own will, the kind of dance where "past and future are gathered." We note, for example, how, "Or say that the end precedes the beginning," (line 148), illustrates the co-existence of what the violin is (earth-enclosed air) and what the violin is for (vibrant air); but the next line, "And the end and the beginning *were always there*" (italics supplied), by the use of the italicized words, shoves these ends and beginnings into a past where as intentions they have eternal life. "Before *the* beginning and after *the* end" (italics supplied). The poet here in the next line produces a doubling reminiscent of the doubling in the rose garden (There they were . . . and we), and the "end" of making these "beginnings" move in a formal pattern is that there is a momentary shaft of sunlight introduced by the "and" signal. "And all is always now" (line 151), brings to a reader a sense of relief and delight as if after great effort the poet has wooed competing children into a place where their passionate voices suddenly rise in one vibrating chord. (Part of this relief may be due to the way we are sent all the way back to lines four and five: "If all time is eternally present/ All time is unredeemable." *This* is how far the protagonist has come.)

Yet it is as if just one glimpse of the real reality is enough to send us back to the jarring actual. Why is this? Is it that the aim of the first half of this stanza has been accomplished: the statement of what words must *do*. Now the poet passes to what the words must suffer if they are to *be* what they must do. A peculiar feature of the new phase is the way it contains a line of the initial bird motif: "Scolding, mocking, or merely chattering" (line 156). "Scolding" and "mocking" is what the thrush *did*—luring us into the garden, then expelling us from it—acting as the agent of our rise and fall. A new image takes its place: "The Word in the desert," what Eliot elsewhere ("Geron-tion") refers to as "The word within a word, unable to speak a word," and (*Ash-Wednesday*) "The Word with-out a word." The submerged contrast seems powerful and effective, as if in the "suffering" phase the poet has found the right words wherewith to be still and still moving. The "crying shadow in the funeral dance," "The loud lament of the disconsolate chimera" are new emblems of "time past" and "time future," what has been and what might have been, the echoes in the corridor and the echoes in the garden. I have the feeling that here the poet seeks to bring to consciousness a condition of being that is utterly different from life in the corridor or life in the garden, a state Harry Monchensey and Agatha half express in *The Family Reunion.*

HARRY: *Look, I do not know why,*
   I feel happy for a moment, as if I had come home.
   It is quite irrational, but now
   I feel quite happy, as if happiness
   Did not consist in getting what one wanted
   Or in getting rid of what can't be got rid of
   But in a different vision. This is like an end.
AGATHA: *And a beginning.*[56]

In stanza one, then, the poet does what words must do and suffers what words must suffer in doing what they must do; therefore he is still and still moving. In stanza two, he transcends words, and though still moving, is still in a new sense.

We may wonder why at this stage of the poem, the poet introduces the new "figure of the ten stairs." Then we may wonder how successful his use of it is. The figure is from the final chapters of St. John of the Cross's *Dark Night of the Soul.*[57] St. John of the Cross took the image from Saint Bernard; it stands for the ladder of contemplation whereby the soul ascends to God. By this figure, and by the words he uses immediately thereafter, the poet interprets the relation of the soul to its ultimate concern in terms that echo many traditional voices both Christian and pagan. A. E. Taylor has suggested [58] that we read Plato's *Symposium* right only when we read it in the light of documents like *The Dark Night of the Soul*. We must hear, not merely the saint's voice, but the philosopher's. Eliot, thus, is giving a very brief but very comprehensive interpretation of the meaning of the soul's "movements." The synoptic vision he offers is not, like that in Section II, a poet's vision, but that of "the mind of Europe." [59] He here then is "eliciting some perception of an order *in* reality, to bring us to a condition of serenity, stillness, and reconciliation." [60]

If we think of *Burnt Norton* as the "air" quartet, Eliot now makes the air vibrant for as far as the ear can hear. And we move with "them" in a new sense. The result? Inspiration descends again, "even while the dust moves," despite, that is, the distraction of an arid physical existence. Or in the words of Josiah Royce, "In the tale here presented, the dust of our natural divisions is stirred into new life. From the tomb of individual banishment into which the divine has freely descended, from the wreck to which every human individual is justly doomed, the Word made flesh arises." [61] The children's voices sound, not as other echoes, but as present reality, and what the deceptive bird said formerly, the poet himself says now (line 175): "Quick now, here, now, always———." And since the poet now finds the "deserts of vast eternity" "ridiculous," his liberation from time seems achieved: he can rejoin the children.

5 CONCLUSION:
VIEW FROM BURNT NORTON

STANDING AT THE THIRD MIDDLE, *Burnt Norton,* and looking backward and forward, certain patterns not visible before are perhaps visible now. The Right Answer, introduced in Chapter 2 to facilitate acceptance of the idea that an absolute reality is indisputable, is merely the world order implicit in every act of perception. The dome of many-colored glass, used in Chapter 2 to focus the aspects of Eliot's world, is merely that world order made explicit. The four-dimensional view of the literary process incorporated in Chapter 3 to interpret Eliot's criticism—language as an act whereby an organ of the universe temporarily dislocated from that universe re-establishes rapport—is merely the rhythm of departure and return in a world order. *Burnt Norton,* a symbolic drama, illustrates the act whereby mankind severs itself from the real reality and then makes that severance a mode of restoration. It is a poet's attempt to re-enact the whole rhythm of language. Thus, the Right Answer would seem to correspond to what F. H. Bradley called a finite center of immediate experience, a knowing and a being at once, which will not leave us but follows us everywhere. The dome of glass corresponds to that total system of experience that Bradley called reality with its appearances. The notion of artistic expression as a four-phase act is merely a translation of the familiar idealistic notion that thought starts with an undifferentiated whole, breaks it up into qualities and relations, objects and subjects, and then strives toward a restored unity where all distinctions are retained. The difficulty with idealistic philosophizing is that a poet is needed to make it credible.

Standing out from Eliot's three "middles," and contemplating a recurrent feature, I am moved by the way Eliot is possessed by the in-between nature of human existence. An absolute reality is certain, but we can only point to it. It operates in us, it operates us, but we are separated from it. Our only relief is to learn to become good pointers. Looking from the third "middle" at the poetry which leads up to *Burnt Norton*, I am struck by how sharply the potential disastrousness of the in-between existence is expressed. Eliot exhibits the desolate dynamics of selves uncentered from their center: time is a masquerade; life a treadmill; existence an interminable pointless circling that grinds deeper and deeper into degradation. Taking account of the poetry on either side of *Burnt Norton*, I am impressed by how works, each of which incorporates a new state of feeling, form one work. This organization of feeling, the business of one poet's lifetime of work, may hardly be appreciated yet. One tentative conclusion may, however, be offered. *Burnt Norton* looks like an important cross-over point in Eliot's life. It marks the point where the poet, momentarily, becomes a public functionary. Up to here, he is a physician whose patient is himself; afterward, the world is his patient. One way to see how that this might be so is to note that up to *Burnt Norton* a significant dissociation exists between the man whose sufferings provide the artist his material and the poet who creates. In "Prufrock" (1910–11), it is Prufrock who is in hell, not the poet. In "The Hippopotamus" (1917), it is the fool who speaks who is in danger of hellfire, not the learned person who contrives the epigraphs. In *The Waste Land* (1922), a margin of safety separates Teresias from the typist whose lost life is the object of contemplation. Even in *The Hollow Men* (1925), where the poet seems to be taking down the last gasps of a human spirit, it is the human spirit that is expiring, not the poetic. Not until *Ash-Wednesday*

(1930), does the poet get caught. Then the man, reborn by the Lady's grace, turns toward the poet for help and finds him blocking the way toward the new life. In *Burnt Norton* (1935), the man corners the poet and destroys him, for the command to descend lower, the equivalent of Prospero's dismissal of Ariel, is a command to be the Word in the world, not merely to speak it. Man and poet coalesce.

If this description of the line of development in Eliot's work up to *Burnt Norton* is valid, *Burnt Norton* marks the place where the poet exhausts his personal material and goes forward to something else. The subsequent *Quartets* having a new material, should show a new form and function. *East Coker* (1940) perhaps provides the first interesting illustration of how this may be so, and *The Dry Salvages* (1941), in an entirely different fashion, the second.

On the surface, *East Coker* looks like a personal drama. ("In my beginning is my end . . . I said to my soul . . . So here I am, in the middle of the way . . .") But under the surface, something quite paradoxical is going on. Eliot has said that the events that culminated in World War II induced in him a doubt as to the validity of his civilization and led to a depression that was like a new emotion. (See, for example, "Last Words," *The Criterion*, XVIII [1938–39], 274, and *The Idea of a Christian Society*, p. 65.) This new emotion is the "death of earth" with which *East Coker* begins. The background of that emotion is perhaps the act of self-sacrifice that terminates *Burnt Norton*. The command to descend lower, there, meant commitment to a station and duties in a specific material world. But now, bound to that material world, which seems to have lost the motive for action, the poet is sickened by its demoralization. His sickness is peculiar. Were he sick himself, in his own body, he could take himself to a hospital. But to what hospital may a congeries of banks and insurance companies be sent? Thus the struggle in *East Coker* is likewise peculiar, being a struggle to accept, to be at-one-with, the unacceptable, the un-one, which is to say with the material being of a worldly civilization.

The peculiarity of the emotion, and the peculiarity of the dramatic struggle make *East Coker* the most "poetic" of Eliot's poems, the one that involves the most "as-if-ing." To express his emotion, and to unfold his struggle for atonement, Eliot develops the metaphor of being-ill-in-the-hospital. By this Eliot can objectify in five acts the phases of the crises: first, the search for the causes of the disease, second, assimilation of the causes, third, acceptance of the fate of being diseased man, fourth, submission to an operation, fifth, convalescence and return home. The metaphor is submerged, as is that of the vacation in *Burnt Norton*, but is, I believe, very much there, the story that Eliot de-emphasizes. But unlike the vacation in *Burnt Norton*, the hospital in *East Coker* is pure fiction, and this makes for a special impression rather analogous to that left by Conrad Aiken's "Mr. Arcularis." Yet, illustrative of the paradox of imaginative life, the fictionality of *East Coker* ultimately results in a sense of great directness, as if the poem were not a poem at all, but real life, *the* state of mind itself. *East Coker* thus illustrates F. H. Bradley's contention ("On Floating Ideas and the Imaginary") that no hard and fast line can be drawn between "real" and "imaginary," or Eliot's in the dissertation (Chapter IV), that the "real" world is an ideal construction.

But even brief analysis of the dramatic progression in *East Coker* seems to support the idea that *East Coker* is a "public" poem, the sufferings not of a physical man, but of a poet taking into himself the illness of his material world. The first act, a journey, is a real journey, yet it is also a fiction, a delirium; yet that delirium is an act, the way dreams are acts, the act of a soul seeking the source of its delirium. We have to say all of these things (as we have to say them of Mr. Arcularis' journey), then we have to say that the sick body, which this soul is probing, is a civilization. "In my beginning is my end," cries the poet, and this cry is like an answer to the soul's unspoken question, but an answer not fully understood. Instantaneously, therefore, the journey begins, as dreams begin. Houses start to rise and fall, imagistic signals of a train journey back to East Coker. These images have the distorted literalism of cinematography. This is the way houses and factories behave when photographed by a camera pointed from the windows of a speeding train. But this landscape is also a metaphor of the poet's "end" from which he starts. This is the nightmare of the twentieth-century material progress that daunted Henry Adams. Disease? Delirium? Cinematic journey? Real act? The opening of *East Coker* is all of these and none. When Eliot's camera shifts to a lane leading to East Coker, a fine shot of the village, dead in electric heat, old stones absorbing not refracting sunlight (we are expected to note the contrast between "my" beginning and "our first world" in *Burnt Norton*), becomes the image of the "beginning" for which the sick soul is searching. But the soul is not at the beginning yet, or not yet *in* the beginning. Eliot manages the phases of the search by manipulating a field image. First, on the outskirts, evidently of London, the camera lingers briefly on "an open field"; in the branch-shuttered lane leading to East Coker, the camera photographs the light falling across "the open field." But the place of the midnight dance around the bonfire is focused as "that open field." The accelerating specificity signals as it were our getting closer and closer to the real beginning, the "venal sin in which our lives began." For the dance represents sexual intercourse. But the real beginning of the disease that climaxes in World War II, is perhaps revealed by the words of Sir Thomas Elyot, whose Tudor voice is dubbed in rather in the pretentious fashion of an art-film. In the anthropocentric renaissance humanism, that confused terrestrial and celestial community, our "end" began. Having reached this beginning, the poet-as-patient suffers a moment of repulsion. "Dung and death," he says and then emerges momentarily from the delirium. He focuses his sick body by the image of dawn at sea and his sick mind by the formula "I am here/ Or there, or elsewhere." Then he makes his first conscious act. "In my beginning," he says, and by cutting in half that phrase with which the poem began, expresses the intention to be wholly in the disease of his beginning.

The poet's first step toward carrying out this intention is an ideal-act, an act, as in *Burnt Norton* of dancing the reality reached in Section I. This he attempts to do by re-dancing (at the start of Section II) the dance around the bonfire (the beginning), as it has come to be in the end (World War II). It is a curious, almost farcical, yet terrifying performance. The up-down, hot-cold contrasts suggest a mind slipping back into delirium; the imagery suggests the farce of a metropolis trying to keep time to constellations that are fleets of enemy bombers. The poet cannot dance this dance. (Again we should note the contrast with *Burnt Norton*.) The poet himself emphasizes the breakdown: "That was a way of putting it . . ." in order that the real struggle to carry out the intention of being "In my beginning" may be visible. It is the struggle to dance the otherwise undanceable by sitting still. We see the poet carrying out his intention by a series of stripping actions. By various devices he strips away the "poetry" from material existence ("the poetry does not *matter*") to become a good materialist, one not taken in by the "wisdom" of "old men" who make stars of uncelestial things and fancy lights of dogs. What he is doing is attuning his mind to the humbleness of matter, the real property of which is to be nothing in itself, merely serviceable matter *for* something. A degree of success is attained, a moment of stillness and lucidity occurs:

> *The houses are all gone under the sea.*
> *The dancers are all gone under the hill.*

At the start of Section III, the end for which the poet has been preparing himself is reached: "O dark, dark, dark./ They all go into the dark." What they do is what the poet had been in danger of doing: abandoning the world's sick body. What the poet does, we assume, is what, previously, he had instructed his soul to do: Sit still. This is the crucial act in the poem (as "descend lower" is in *Burnt Norton*).

But the acceptance of the destiny of disease in Section III leads to the atoning operation in Section IV. The hymn-like lyric is a daring piece of rhetoric, aiming perhaps to bring out in contemporary terms the "scandal" of the cross, and its verity. The metaphor of the wounded surgeon is an example of Eliot's continuous realistic fictionality. For the scalpel the physician wields must be Nazi armament, and the surgeon, Christ the Tiger. To be able to word the predicament thus is almost tantamount to being at-one with it.

Having stripped himself of "poetry" in Section II, the convalescent poet, in Section V, pictures himself putting on his poetic clothing again, preparatory to going "home." Curiously, but appropriately, he puts on what a materialistic world has to offer. He speaks of himself and his poetic vocation with terms drawn from a capitalistic economy. He uses the words "new start," "failure," "get the better of," "venture," "shabby equipment," "conditions . . . unpropitious," and the last word he speaks in the first stanza is "business." What we watch for is a sign of chafing against his destiny. But the poet's behaviour is as matter of fact as Eggerson's in *The Confidential Clerk*, who speaks the Word while using clichés. In the second stanza of Section V, "home" is now the very condition that had heretofore been the sign of disease: to be here, there, and everywhere, to be at sea. Thus the poet can reverse the formula and say, "In my end is my beginning."

Analysis of *East Coker*, then, seems to support the idea that *Burnt Norton* is the end of the poet as a person. The poet's "matter" in *East Coker* is the sickness of a world. In a second, quite different fashion *The Dry Salvages* also illustrates the public character of Eliot's poetry after *Burnt Norton*. The poem has actually been undervalued by interpreters failing to see that the public role the poet plays in this is a key to the form. The role is that of the poet-as-preacher, and in approaching it, we need to remember that the sermon, as Eliot once remarked (*The Athenaeum*, "The Preacher as Artist," November 28, 1919) is, perhaps, the most difficult of art forms. It is an intensely dramatic genre, the struggle between preacher and congregation being, like that between a snake charmer and his snake, dangerous. For though a man playing a flute to a reptile may look and sound like a comic character, we get a different impression if we look at his eyes. If he fails in his art, the snake may destroy him. A congregation, released from the complaisances of a weekday routine, is a collective consciousness looking down from above on a life unaccountably lost in the living. It is a group mind that, like nature, mourns for a lost good, and easily turns demonic. A great preacher (who probably should not ever speak loud or long) mediates between three orders, the demonic, the human, and the divine, and if he succeeds in his calling, does so by being a man of the world with a strong sense of humor. Two famous fictional representations of the preacher in American literature illustrate two ways in which the preacher may fail. Hawthorne's Reverend Arthur Dimmesdale is not a great preacher because he is too much enraptured by the divine; he and we know why this is so. Melville's Father Mapple is too afraid of the demonic. Neither is a free human person such as Kierkegaard attempted to sketch in his description of the Knight of Faith or Eliot himself tried to project in *The Cocktail Party* in Sir Henry Harcourt-Reilly. Whatever we may think of that latter figure (and he does, as Bertrand Russell once said of Socrates, sometimes speak like an Anglican cleric of the bad type) we begin to get hold of the form of *The Dry Salvages* better when we see that Eliot in it is one of the "guardians," a Yankee Harcourt-Reilly. He is sociable, colloquial, loquacious, and bungling, a Connecticut Yankee whose hymn to the Virgin shows him to be incapable of carrying a tune. But the comic *persona* does not affect the fact that a potentially tragic struggle is going on.

The struggle in *The Dry Salvages* is to deal with "the agony of others." An ex-millionaire in a concentration camp might testify that it is easier to say goodbye to property than to speak to the agony of others, especially if these include people we care about. What is needed is not an expression of sympathy, which is useless, nor a promise of relief, which does not exist, nor a lesson in stoicism, which plays into the hands of the enemy, but a dialogue, the kind that Krishna engages Arjuna in on the field of battle and that gives him his freedom. Such a dialogue, makes a game of human suffering.

Such a dialogue tests the skill of the preacher. We see Eliot attempting it in Section I of *The Dry Salvages*. He starts by calling attention to himself so that his hearers will see and disregard that self. Later, all of his important utterances are but transmissions from another source, as in Section III where it is the wireless aerial that gives the command to fare forward. The preacher begins quietly, using the vocabulary of the congregation, focusing the river, that strong brown god, first from the shore position, then from the river's position, then, becoming a poet and evoking childhood memories, and entering the river by entering its rhythm. Having got the congregation itself inside it, he then places that river inside them and goes on. This strong brown god, it goes without saying, is the congregation on the verge of plunging into the ocean. We note that the poet-protagonist goes out to meet that collective entity, but not to be it. His significant action all takes place in an air-space that he controls.

The preacher next confronts the sea, and his maneuverings follow the same pattern as before. He confronts that watery body's alienness to shore from a shore position, and then its hostility to shore from a sea position. Then he takes account of the spiritual dimension of this element, the many gods and many voices. But before entering with his congregation into that dangerous dimension, he reminds them that their encounter with the sea is in idea only, the trial and judgment of the sea having already occurred. (At least so I read: "The salt is

on the briar rose/ The fog is in the fir trees.") Having
done this, the preacher standing, up to this time, at the
river's mouth, suddenly casts himself and his hearers far
out to sea; we find ourselves entering the "sea howl,"
"sea yelp," "whine in the rigging," etc. And when we
get our bearings again, we are beating a way back to the
river's mouth. What is the logic of the Preacher's navi-
gation? He is reviving the experiences of sexual life in
their meaning, and just as he went to childhood to get
the river's rhythm, here he goes to adult sexuality for
the river's participation in the sea's life. And just as,
having taken us inside the river, he then put the river
inside us, so now having entered upon the ocean, he
now puts the ocean all around us permanently. He does
so by becoming the anxious worried women whose preg-
nancies cause them to seek "to unweave, unwind, un-
ravel/ And piece together the past and the future."
Though their bodies are on the rocks, their souls are at
sea; meanwhile, in the foetal life inside them, the river
is starting another life cycle. By saying that the women's
souls are at sea, I mean that they have lost faith that
their biological lives are going anywhere, which means
that for them the "death by water" has occurred.

To revive the experience of this specific hell is evidently the first step in the preacher's dialogue with a
congregation. The second step follows almost immediately; it is the asking of the "overwhelming question."
"Where is the end of it?", the preacher cries, at the start
of Section II, almost as if, not he, but his congregation's
voice is raising the question. The dialogue that follows
is forced into a strait jacket of the sestina, a verse pattern so artificial in English as to be rare, and the man-
agement of it, according to one critic at least, is un-
couth. But what the preacher perhaps is giving is the
equivalent of the professionally performed choric dances
found in the second sections of *Burnt Norton* and *East
Coker*. His external form is mimetic of the circles of
despair that the worried anxious women are going
through. His form has the merit of enabling him and

them to keep on going, to keep faring forward even when life cycles are seen to be pointless. The form, in addition, has another virtue. It imitates the one thing that the preacher can do for the agony of others. He can make them make a game of it, and by so doing not only enable the soul to get its terrible questions into the open, but enable the mind to offer its realistic but valueless answers. Thus when the One Annunciation comes, a place in the collective conscience has been prepared for it. And as soon as that answer is given, the congregation is rescued. Thus the voice of the preacher returns, relaxed, amiably indifferent to syntax, and engaged now in reversing the trend. The congregation having moved from disaster to illumination, the preacher moves from illumination back to disaster. This is his way of keeping the agony in its meaning.

Perhaps enough has been said to make plausible the idea that after *Burnt Norton*, by virtue of the act symbolically enacted in *Burnt Norton*, Eliot becomes a public poet going out in *East Coker* and *The Dry Salvages* to meet the destructive conflicts of his world to transform them into fructifying tensions. These poems are Eliot's most satisfying triumphs of literary imagination.

Of the greatest of the *Four Quartets*, *Little Gidding*, not much can be said, briefly, except that in this poem, which both exemplifies and transcends the pattern spoken of, the role of the poet seems to become that of ordinary-man-as-saint. At the end of *The Dry Salvages*, preacher and congregation go home content to acknowledge the difference between what the saints do and what most of us can do. But in *Little Gidding*, circumstances of modern warfare seem to have levelled the distinctions and "We only live, only suspire/ Consumed by either fire or fire." The poet's struggle is to see how, as an ordinary citizen, he can say yes to what looks like the destruction of his spiritual world. The perfection of *Little Gidding* arises from the way that the poet manages to preserve an attitude of intense serenity while not minimizing the intensity of the struggle. The logic of his attitude, perhaps, is that when saints are saints, they are such by virtue of an enlightenment that dissolves all alternatives. The poet gets his enlightenment by going back to Little Gidding, that place where a former world of the spirit was destroyed. And the poet acts out his enlightenment when the ghost of Jonathan Swift arrives to scatter the gifts reserved for the human tongue, and the poet dances that destructive colloquy so well that Swift becomes the agent of the conclusive self-sacrifice that the poet might otherwise have denied. The artist here illustrates the saint's "use" in the world: he shows how to love. Of this passage, which must be one of the high points in Eliot, we may be moved to say of Eliot what he once said of Henry James:

> The example which Henry James offered us was not that of a style to imitate, but of an integrity so great, a vision so exacting, that it was forced to the extreme of care and punctiliousness for exact expression. James did not provide us with "ideas," but with another world of thought and feeling. For such a world some have gone to Dostoievsky, some to James; and I am inclined to think that the spirit of James, so much less violent, with so much more reasonableness and so much more resignation than that of the Russian, is no less profound, and is more useful, more applicable, for our future. ["A Prediction in Regard to Three English Authors," *Vanity Fair* (February 1924), 29.]

6 APPENDIX:
THE WASTE LAND

IF Eliot's beginning as a poet is a metaphysical perspective, *The Waste Land* is a logical end of that specific beginning, the crown of Eliot's preparatory poetic, philosophic and critical labours. It has been passed over in this study because—so the argument went—it never quite becomes a public poem. The question as to whether this is so is not without critical interest.

The difficulties that *The Waste Land* presents are of two sorts. First are those that are due to *The Waste Land*'s being an esoteric poem. A critic is prepared to deal with these because, in a sense, all tragic literature is esoteric. All literature that reveals an eternal order in an everyday existence is explicable only to those inside a circle; it is the critic's job to move in and out of that circle, bringing from the outside those who wish to come in. As Northrop Frye has said, "Criticism can talk, and all the arts are dumb." [1]

The second difficulty is different: *The Waste Land* is Eliot's *Hamlet*. It appears to involve an intense private, perhaps pathological, experience that the author was compelled to express but could not readily objectify inasmuch as the emotion exceeded the facts. *The Family Reunion* has somewhat the same atmosphere, and Harry's reiterated complaints [2] that there is no language for a concrete experience is Eliot's confession of bafflement. That *The Waste Land* expresses a good deal more than one man's private despair no one would deny. That the poem lives on three levels—the personal, the historical, and the racial—seems fairly obvious. It expresses, for example, one man's misfortune, one generation's calamity, and then, something vaster, everyman's encounter with that which in *The Family Reunion* is referred to as "some huge disaster/ Some monstrous mistake and aberration/ Of all men, of the world, which I cannot put in order." [3]

That *The Waste Land* made contact with most readers on the second level seems a safe conclusion. Public sources of standardized information tell us that *The Waste Land* attained fame as an expression of the disillusionment of a generation. It seems fitting that the poem, having thus come to occupy a position as a monumental memorial to the "lost generation," should now seem dated. (The poem is not dated; its public image is.) This being so, it is also understandable why, ten years after the poem had made him notable, Eliot dismissed the public image of his poem as "nonsense." [4] All truths that are true, Eliot once said in his dissertation, are private truths; when they become public formulas, they are catchwords and false. Later Eliot insisted that he wrote the poem to express emotions of his own. [5]

Eliot's insistence that he wrote the poem to express *his* state of mind, however, involves an important point. The life of the poem derives from the way (to lift out of context a statement Eliot made about Shakespeare and Dante) the poet has attempted "to fabricate something permanent and holy out of his personal animal feelings . . . to transmute his personal and private agonies into something rich and strange, something universal and impersonal." [6] Eliot's procedure in *The Waste Land* is to make a riddle of his personal experience by relating it in terms of historical and racial experiences of other men. The chaos of a world functions to mirror the protagonist's blind intentions and to compel self-recognition and self-reversal. To think that *The Waste Land* is about the way (after the "breakdown of standards") young men carbuncular sleep with typists home at tea-time on divans piled high with stockings, camisoles, and stays is to think that *Lear* is about a storm on a heath.

But to return to what Eliot wrote *The Waste Land* for is to return to the second difficulty: a poem lives somewhere between something that it is coming *from* and something that it is going *toward*. In *The Waste Land* it seems hard to tell what the poem is moving from. In literature the mind thinks with the body and we have to know where to put it. Mostly we assimilate this automatically. In Donne's "The Ecstasy" or Keats's "Ode to a Nightingale" we react to the signals and are under way. But not in *The Waste Land*. Eliot expects us to sit like Japanese before a Noh play, recognizing that that folded pink kimona draped over a chair [7] is all the information we are going to get about the protagonist's physiological circumstances: he is sexually dead like the Fisher King. And Eliot is perhaps right to force our imaginations.

Having appeared to reason myself out of the validity of the second difficulty (but not the sense of difficulty), I come now to the point of this Appendix. *The Waste Land* presents itself as a challenge to any one who comes to it after investigating the importance of Eliot's three "middles." If the hypotheses argued for have substance, we should come to *The Waste Land* with new eyes. Do we? The answers, unfortunately or fortunately, are Yes and No. We see certain things with greater ease. But the materials, or many of them, remain as mysterious as before, and it probably is a good thing that poems should defeat critical strategies for taking them captive.

Despite this, however, to come to *The Waste Land* from *Burnt Norton*, from the early criticism, from the treatise on F. H. Bradley is to see one virtue of the poem that has never adequately been appreciated. It is, however difficult was its birth, a triumph of design. Critics who have thought otherwise must be dead wrong. Ezra Pound's groan of envious admiration must be taken as tribute to the formal achievement. [8]

To see the design of *The Waste Land*, however, requires us to think in dramatic terms. It is an imitation of an action; it has a beginning, middle, and end, five acts, five characters (more or less) and a stage manager. Teresias, a "personage," Eliot says, not a character, fulfills more or less the function of a Greek Chorus as that is conceived by Nietzsche in *The Birth of Tragedy*.[9] Teresias mediates between us and the protagonist; he enables us to see the god struggling to be born in the man. He defines the metaphysical point of view. The beginning is one of those turns of time that Nietzsche called the "jeopardy of the will,"[10] a place where the soul's dilemma is so great it will extinguish itself unless art comes to the rescue, and the ending is a point of impossible reconciliation where, in Eliot's words, "That is the completion which at the beginning/ Would have seemed the ruin."[11]

Eliot has done a number of interesting things, I believe, to help us see the "plot" of *The Waste Land* while doing everything in his power to draw the "hypocrite lecteur" away from the "story." One such device is his use of tenses. Verb tenses are usually crucial in Eliot and in *The Waste Land* they are important stage signals as to the whereabouts of the action. The classic pattern in much great tragedy is illustrated by a formula to be found in Eliot's *Dry Salvages*: "And the way up is the way down, the way forward is the way back." In *The Waste Land*, as in *Oedipus Rex* and *Death of a Salesman* (to go from extreme to extreme) the protagonist is caught in a present that is in the grip of the past, and the past keeps erupting into the present demanding acknowledgment and acceptance of an entity that is always now. To investigate Eliot's verbs, strange as it may seem, is to investigate his action.

"The Burial of the Dead," Section I of *The Waste Land*, begins in the present tense: "April *is* the cruelest month," then almost immediately slides back into the past: "Winter *kept* us warm," "Summer *surprised* us." Yet (at the end of the first scene) the tenses glide upward toward an historical present: "I *read* much of the night" which then fuses with the ambiguous opening of Scene 2: "What *are* the roots that clutch?" which in turn becomes firmly grounded in the *now* of "Son of man, you *cannot* say, for you *know*," etc. The Hyacinth Garden episode that follows is firmly planted in an exact past time: "You *gave* me hyacinths first a year ago" (last April). And so is the visit to Madam Sosostris who "*had* a bad cold" (last winter). The "Unreal City" episode, time—dawn, season—winter, is past tense. "A crowd *flowed* over London Bridge," "I *had* not thought," "There I *saw* one I knew." But the concluding lines of the section make a violent entrance into the present time. "You! hypocrite lecteur!—mon semblable,—mon frere!" Cutting across these tenses—irrelevant to the time sequence—but very relevant to the timeless core of the action in Section I are three imperatives: "Come in under the shadow of this red rock," "Fear death by water," and "Keep the dog far hence." These commands make Eliot's stage bristle with action.

"The Game of Chess" (Section II), "The Fire Sermon" (Section III), and "Death By Water" (Section IV) are for the most part fixed in past time, except for the concluding lines in each section where the grammar, as it were, forces us back into the present crisis: "Good night, ladies," "O Lord thou pluckest/ burning," and "Consider Phlebas." Section III (the puzzling "middle") has erratic tenses: "The river's tent *is* broken" (despite the autumn setting) in contrast to "By the waters of Leman I *sat* down and *wept*" in contrast to "But at my back in a cold blast I hear" in contrast to "A rat *crept*" (winter). Mr. Eugenides issues his invitation in a clearly marked past time—"*Asked* me in demotic French"—but the seduction of the typist is described in present tense, perhaps because to be conscious with Teresias of action is not to be in time.

Section IV is all past. "Phlebas . . . *Forgot*." But Section V erupts into the present and the effect is as though after some delay there is actual *action*. Eliot reinforces this impression by use of setting: it must be

Easter (April) and an April that is hot and dry (like summer), in a place that duplicates that at the beginning where Teresias commands: "Come in under the shadow of this red rock." This locale is the setting of the present crisis in the poem. In Section V, Eliot holds a steady present tense straight through the first six stanzas —with one exception, the fifth. This is the longest stretch of present tense in the poem. It is as if, with notice of the death of Phlebas, the Quester is born and we watch him move (at the end of the day) across the desert plain at the base of the mountains, to arrive at night at the Chapel Perilous. Then something peculiar occurs. The cock crows, and the Thunder speaks, but the voice of God speaks in past tense. This contrast, if we watch for it, is startling, and we are drawn to seek explanations in order to realize, perhaps, that the way forward *is* the way back, and that this judgment did occur in the past, but the protagonist did not hear it. Now he does, and this is the important break-through in his life. In short, the Thunder spoke, and man did not hear it, though he lived what it spoke, and having lived it, now re-utters the judgment to himself for himself.

The tenses in the coda are fascinating. We see the Fisher King fishing in past tense (yet with the arid plain *behind* him), and we see him using one of the few simple futures of the poem "*Shall* I at least set my lands in order?" (The others occur in "The Game of Chess.") When the battery of fragments explodes, it is hard to tell where we are. I am inclined to say we are in a past that is in the process of being accepted and so is present.

My purpose is not so much to explicate *The Waste Land* as to speak of certain external features that carefully attended to lead rather far into the form of the poem. The pronouns, like the verb tenses, are very important. There are five of them—I, you, we, she, and they. There are ambiguities, but for the most part the "I" is the "eye-seeing" of the protagonist, the protagonist as subject; the "you" is the protagonist as object. Eliot is very careful of his "you"—understandably so since it is the crucial character in his drama. It figures prominently in the other person's discourse, the *other* who is looking at the protagonist. "*You* gave me hyacinths first a year ago." "Here is *your* card." "Do *you* know nothing?" But it figures also at the climax of the poem when the protagonist crossing the desert turns (as I see it) and addresses himself (italics supplied):

> *Who is the third who walks always beside* you?
> *When I count, there are only* you *and I together*
> *But when I look ahead up the white road*
> *There is always another one walking beside* you.

When the protagonist is talking to his apparent other, the woman, he almost never addresses her directly with the pronoun "you." He speaks of "we" and "I," or he thinks of her in the third person as "she." The protagonist will use "you" to address Stetson, "You who were with me in the ships at Mylae!" or the reader, "You! hypocrite lecteur!" or again "O you who turn the wheel and look to windward"; only once will he use "your" to refer to the girl: "Your arms full, and your hair wet." This is his affliction. He sees her only once as he sees himself. At the Thunder's judgment, a climactic moment in the poem, the pronouns march, drag, and creep onto the stage to receive their condemnation, and in the three judgments we see that *Datta* (Give) involves "we," *Dayadhvam* (sympathize) involves "I," and most pathetic of all *Damyata* (control) involves "you," scarcely visible amidst the poet's ship imagery (italics supplied):

> Damyata: *The boat responded*
> *Gaily, to the hand expert with sail and oar*
> *The sea was calm*, your *heart would have responded*
> *Gaily, when invited, beating obedient*
> *To controlling hands.*

If "you" in the poem designates the protagonist's "me," the protagonist's affliction is that it is dead. The *agon* in the poem is his struggle to see and come to terms with this fact.

A third way that Eliot calls attention to his bold, simple design is by the use of stage properties. Eliot's imagination is not unlike Eugene O'Neill's. Both are visualizers. Someone should compare the formal pattern of *Emperor Jones* and *The Waste Land*, not because there was necessarily influence, but because both men saw actions unfolding in what Blake would call a psychic landscape. Eliot's plot begins on middle ground, on a flat plain, at the base of the *Rock*; but his protagonist looks back to a starting point "in the mountains" where "you feel free." We follow the action (after two trips up and down a pair of stairs) down the Thames with the Thames Maidens and then down into the depths of ocean with Phlebas, "entering the whirlpool." In Section V, "you and I" start climbing again, moving eastward to the Himalayas and another river (the sacred Ganges). There at the Chapel Perilous the "you" evidently is finally lost, or is recognized perhaps to have been lost long ago. At the end of the poem, the Fisher King sits facing the sea with the arid plain behind him. But the mountains, rock, plain, river, ocean, plain, mountains are stage properties that call attention to the V-shape of the action. This is a tragic or mythic action where, in contrast to the A-shape of heroic legend, the action starts high, falls low and then climbs high again. (This is the pattern of *Paradise Lost–Paradise Regained* that was exemplified in *Burnt Norton*.)

Verbs, pronouns, stage "props" are all things easily seen. A fourth feature, also quite visible, leads us into something that is not a device but an organizing method in the poem. Everyone must have noticed how frequently in *The Waste Land* sequences tend to come in threes. Three Thames maidens lament their fall, three judgments are pronounced by the Thunder on the protagonist, three fragments are shored by him against his ruins. There are of course other sequences: runs of four, runs of five, pairs. And I am not sure that Eliot's runs of three do not always (like Beethoven's much exploited theme of fate in the Fifth Symphony) involve a fourth note, explicitly or implicitly. But for simplicity's sake I shall say that the basic principle of design in *The Waste Land* is the triad. If this is so, it is interesting, because it suggests that Eliot, in struggling to organize his experiences, may quite consciously have employed, or exploited for poetic purposes, something very like Bradley's dialectical method,[12] an essentially Hegelian method which Josiah Royce, following (not Hegel) but Charles Peirce, formulated in his own interesting way in *The World and the Individual* (1900–1901) and again in *The Problem of Christianity* (1913). I would suspect that it was Royce primarily who led Eliot to see the poetic possibilities of the principle of interpretation. Very briefly Royce's principle is this: where two entities collide and clash, we must find a third entity to put "between" them in order to reveal the ground of identity omnipresent even in things unlike.[13] Let me try to show how the Royce principle of interpretation could be applied in a reading of the beginning and end of *The Waste Land*.

Section I, "The Burial of the Dead" begins in present tense, in the voice of the "I." But after four lines we pass from present to past, from this April to last winter, then to summer. Summer is the Third that completes the first triad. It reveals the ground of identity in occasions seemingly different. But the revelation does not come through. The summer motif, therefore, is repeated. As a result a new contrast breaks out, *our* summer (1) conveyed largely by visual images ("Summer surprised *us,* coming over the Starnbergersee"), and *their* summer experience (2) ("Bin gar keine Russin, stamm' aus Litauen, echt deutsch") conveyed by auditory images. The first is what we saw ourselves experiencing; the second is what we heard some other saying she experienced in her moment of reality. The "I" remembers both, but the point of the juxtaposition is that these opposites are the same. That is to say, the meaning of our summer is revealed by what Marie said. But this revelation also fails to break through. The sequence is terminated and a new stanza begins. This stanza starts a new series. But if we hold just a moment to the last two halves of Stanza 1 and listen to the start of Stanza 2, "What are the roots that clutch, what branches grow/ Out of *this* stony rubbish?" (italics supplied) we are getting the Third that interprets the two halves of the Munich summer scene. Let us go back over Stanza 1 to see how this is so.

If we run through the sequence of (1) April, (2) winter, (3) Munich in summer, and attempt to label the 1, 2, and 3, we might come up with something like (1) unpeaceful death (the dead land breeding lilacs), (2) peaceful death (dry tubers under forgetful snow), and (3) peaceful life (sunlight, rain, conversation; there is no I-you contrast, no male-female; merely *us* and *we* receiving something and doing something together, talking together). But the point that should emerge from the re-enactment in memory of the good summer, is that the same shadow over-shadows what the protagonist experienced then as good as what he experiences now as the worst evil. Since he does not see the shadow across *his* summer actions, the summer memory knocks on the door again with the overheard conversation. There is no indication that he yet comprehends and so the harsh voice of the Stranger (Teresias) breaks in, "What are the roots that clutch, what branches grow/ Out of this stony rubbish?" Then *we* see the Shadow in the Hofgarten. The voice of Marie (recollected in this April's torment) speaks of a fall from freedom and delight brought about evidently by a natural desire to retain freedom and delight. The voice of Marie, I am arguing, given this protagonist in this predicament, identifies the motive that has to be purged, what in the analysis of *Burnt Norton* was called aestheticism—the desire to pluck experience without reference to its meaning. Marie's final line, "I read, much of the night, and go south in the winter" seems to support the point, though it is not until the poet turns on us in the final line of Section I, "You! hypocrite lecteur" that we see how *his* and *our* aestheticism may be a "deadly error." [14]

The second stanza sets before us two contrasting visual scenes and two contrasting scraps of music. The basic internal contrast is between Teresias' desert (1) and Belladonna's garden (2). The basic external contrast is between the Hyacinth garden (2) and the Hofgarten (1) in the preceding stanza. The longer the poem un-rolls, the more complicated the dialectic seems to be-come. So, in Stanza 2, the two fragments of music from the beginning and end of Wagner's *Tristan and Isolde* frame the Hyacinth garden and perform the function of double Thirds that reveal the ground of identity between Teresias' desert (1) and Belladonna's garden (2), and Hyacinth garden (2) and Hofgarten (1). Let us see how this might be so.

In the command of Teresias to come in under the shadow of this red rock, we have the command that converts desert into garden and garden into desert. The protagonist will obey before the poem is over. What does the command mean? It means for the protagonist to cease to think of his life "as an isolated ruin," and to begin to see it as part of a "huge disaster"—to see it as involved in the "doom on the world." [15] Why does Teresias' desert utterance get jammed against Bella-donna's, "You gave me hyacinths first a year ago"? It does, we may assume, because the demand that Teresias confronts the protagonist with *this* April contains a fea-ture that is identical with the demand made upon him last April. The agony in the desert, the ecstasy in the garden are alike in that they involve encounters with a supernatural reality that the protagonist can not respond to. Desert and garden are places, therefore, of supernat-ural terror. The poet shies away from this April to last April to show why he can not obey Teresias.

This reading of the Hyacinth garden episode may seem (like the reading of the Marie episode) somewhat arbitrary unless we agree to take it as one element in a series of elements. Once Eliot spoke of Dante as attempting to give us the most ordered presentation of emotions ever attempted.[16] The same end motivates Eliot in *The Waste Land*. Marie's mountain adventure is happiness; the protagonist's Hyacinth garden experience is an encounter with the "real reality" (the "heart of light"—cf. *Burnt Norton*) and therefore "ecstatic," but it is the ecstasy of one who has no form whereby to reach that reality. It is the ecstasy of one in Hell, as the Third—Wagner's music—should make plain. Tristan's love of Isolde is evoked, that complex image of romantic love, love, that is to say, cut off from its origin and end, love become essentially solitary. As Jean Guitton states in *Essay on Human Love*, Stendhal, Proust, Freud, Sartre all exorcise the existence of the *other* from love.[17] So, I should say, does Wagner. What Guitton states with respect to Proust could be said of Wagner: "the beloved is an illusion created by human art, reflecting back upon the man his own image." For Eliot's protagonist, too, there is no real *other* through whom love can be made real in act. The Hyacinth Girl thinks that there has been a real giving and taking, but the protagonist's negative "yet" disabuses us of this illusion. And the night setting of the episode (which contrasts with the bright sun of the Hofgarten) causes us to think of Blake's

> God appears, and God is light
> To those poor souls who dwell in night,
> But doth a human form display
> To those who dwell in realms of day.

But the Wagner Third in Stanza 2 interprets not only the apparent contrast of Teresias' red rock and Belladonna's rocks, but the contrast of the Hyacinth garden and the Hofgarten. What Wagner mistakenly glorifies in *Tristan and Isolde* is the aesthetizing of human life. By putting Wagner *between* Hofgarten (1) and Hyacinth garden (2) the protagonist acknowledges the beginning and end of his own aesthetizing of life. A fancy way to say this is that gardens in Eliot are always places of birth and death, and that in the Hofgarten the man died and the poet was born and that in the Hyacinth garden the poet was slain and the man was reborn. Destroying the poet in the Hyacinth garden is the realization that disembodied love (such as Wagner celebrates) is intolerable.

Stanza 3 is a curious one—a comic scene—or so it seems if we put it over against the torments of Stanzas 1 and 2. Consider the contrast between "April is the cruelest month," "What are the roots that clutch?" and "Madam Sosostris had a bad cold/ Nevertheless. . . ." That *nevertheless* has been said to be a long-drawn-out snuffle. To pass from Teresias' prophetic voice to the snuffle of the Madam is to set up a new contrast demanding interpretation. Here the organization of the poem might be visualized in two ways. Standing in Madam Sosostris' parlor and contrasting her voice with that of Teresias crying in the Wilderness, we might look for a new Third to mediate the contrast. Or noting that Madam Sosostris' stanza is the last in a sequence of three we might look to Stanza 4 as the doubled Third that brings about the insight that Stanza 3 does not produce. Either way, we look to Stanza 4 for the revelation that fuses all the preceding ones. The pattern of "The Burial of the Dead" might be thought of as a rhythm: One, two, three, THREE, or knock, knock, knock, KNOCK. And if the idea is not too fanciful, the rhythm seems to define two seasonal sequences, one bringing to light the death that lurked in summer, one disclosing the life struggling to emerge from winter. The pattern looks like this:

Stanza 1: (1) *April*, (2) *Winter*, (3) *Summer*, (4) SUMMER.
Stanzas
2, 3, 4:   (1) *April*, (2) *April*,   (3) *Winter*, (4) WINTER.

But to come back to the position of Stanza 3 in the dialectic of the poem, What happens in the house of Madam Sosostris? The protagonist gets his fortune told; yet that, as Sweeney might say, does not signify. We need to keep the scene on the stage. Madam Sosostris seems to be sought out last winter in contrast to Teresias who is met with this April. The interview is something that the protagonist re-enacts in memory now. To what point in his history does he go back when he goes back to Sosostris? And why in *this* April is he compelled to go back to that point?

The first question raises the problem of the time scheme in the poem as a whole, with special reference to the sequence of events on one winter day. For the sake of an analysis, let me assume that all the winter events occurred in a twenty-four hour period and that the visit to Sosostris was before the beginning of the fateful day that put an end to our winter sleep. Sosostris must be consulted then the night before the shortest day of the year (mid-winter spring of *Little Gidding*); Stetson's ghost is met at dawn, Mr. Eugenides at noon, the typist seduced at sundown, and the news of Phlebas's drowning received that night.

What compels the protagonist to go back in memory to Sosostris? The answer to this question is in the dialectic. Teresias presents the poet with a command that he can neither obey nor not obey; Teresias commands him to suffer what looks like spiritual death. Unable to fare forward or stand still, the poet leaps in memory back to another occasion when filled with distress and perplexity, he consulted another prophet in order to "riddle the inevitable/ With playing cards." (*The Dry Salvages.*) Madam Sosostris had the right cards; she put them on the table: "Here is your card . . . the drowned Phoenician sailor. . . . Here is Belladonna. . . . Fear death by water!" But what she warned against had already happened. This is why the poet rehearses the scene as comedy. But what happened? Who or what is Phlebas, the drowned Phoenician sailor?

We have in Phlebas the point of intersection of three levels of meaning: the racial, the historical, and the personal. On the racial level, he is Tammuz, Adonis, Attis, Osiris, which is to say he is the personification of every-

thing desirable in natural man, that superb natural creature whose strange destiny (as illustrated by the mystery
religions) is never to fulfill his promise, never to answer
his mother-wife's longings, always to suffer unmanning,
death, and resurrection. On the historical level, he is the
renaissance naturalism that, starting from the assumption that natural man is sound substantial flesh and
blood, set forth on the modern adventure that culminated in the blood bath of 1914–18, in which the flower
of Europe perished. On the personal level, he is, if imagination is permissible, perhaps the poet's image of his
youth as it was reflected back to him by the friend who
in 1911 came "across the Luxembourg Gardens in the
late afternoon, waving a branch of lilac," a friend to
whom the 1917 poems were dedicated, and who so far
as Eliot could find out was "to be mixed with the mud of
Gallipoli" in 1915.[18] Phlebas, in short, is that image of
youthful freedom and delight that makes the protagonist
a poet, just as it is the poet who makes the man in the
Hyacinth Garden unable to speak, looking into the heart
of light. So long as the possibility exists that this image
can live, the protagonist can winter his crisis. But if it
cannot, then the bottom, as Peter Quilpe says, in *The
Cocktail Party*, drops out of everything. The protagonist's visit to Sosostris coincides with the night that the
"distress of nations" gave him his first inkling that there
may be an abyss in life from which is no escape.

But to return to the dialectical pattern, though
Madam Sosostris held the cards, she (unlike Teresias)
had no sense of the present to which those cards were
applicable, either with respect to the protagonist or herself. The end of her advice is that "one must be so careful." O God, woman, Harry Monchensey might have
answered, "The things that are going to happen have already happened."

Stanza 4, the climax of Section I, is an extraordinary
piece of design. We have to see the setting: past tense,
winter dawn, the unreal city, the Jolly Corner where
the spectres show themselves. The scene pairs with the

preceding. It is the doubled Third that interprets Stanzas 1 and 2. It consists of three encounters, three recognitions, and a climactic exorcism of the dead spirit (the poet in the protagonist) who must be put to rest if the drama is to go forward and who, as in *Burnt Norton*, is buried by the Poet above the poet.

The first encounter is with *them*, the crowd flowing over London Bridge; the point of importance is not that they are dead, but that in their living death in the urban Limbo, they mirror the face of the poet-protagonist; they are the outward manifestation of what he intended in the Hofgarten (the beginning) without quite realizing what he intended. The second encounter is with Stetson: "You who were with me in the ships at Mylae!" (Is that "Mylae" in there for any other reason than to suggest Carthage, a Phoenician city, and to facilitate identification of Stetson as Phlebas?) But the point of importance is "That corpse *you* planted last year in *your* garden" (italics supplied). This moment suddenly fuses with that moment outside the Hyacinth garden. The poetic, self-regardful principle (the sailor), is now recognized to have buried the possibility of a merely natural relation with the merely natural. (Compare Celia's: "I couldn't give anyone the kind of love/ I wish I could—which belongs to that life" and "You see, I think I really had a vision of something.") [19] This second recognition is the recognition of the "middle" of the action. The third recognition (the end) split into two parts. The protagonist cries out involuntarily:

> Oh keep the Dog far hence, that's friend to men,
> Or with his nails he'll dig it up again!

The imperative mood signifies that he has joined the prophets: his command is the Third between Teresias' "Come in under the shadow of this red rock" and Sosostris's "Fear death by water," which are incompatible. The protagonist's command to his "card" should enable the protagonist to reconcile these seemingly incompatible imperatives. How? Who is the Dog? Many glosses have been offered on Eliot's Dog: he is humanitarianism and bad, he is the Hound of Heaven and hence good, etc. But he is first and foremost a motif in another sequence of three. Is he not, then, the Third that links those in Limbo to Stetson? We do not know him until the "Hypocrite lecteur" arrives; then we do. The *hypocrite lecteur, hypocrite auteur*, alias Stetson, alias Phlebas, alias Ferdinand the Archduke is the poetic principle that preserves life, not that it may live, but that taste may be gratified. The final line, echoing Baudelaire's climactic disgust, slays the Dog, and we have the third death in the "Burial of the Dead." This event, occurring in the wasteland of the modern city, makes the Unreal City a more fertile garden for the protagonist than either Hofgarten or Hyacinth garden.

Many readers have taken *The Waste Land* to be a chaotic and negative poem. Classic art is never really either and *The Waste Land* is a classic work. It is, of course, to repeat my thesis, a philosophic poem in a context of widespread unbelief. But it is a philosophic poem that never philosophizes. By adherence to a firm metaphysical standpoint it discloses the context of order implied by a context of disorder. By a conscious dialectical method it reveals the God above the god that Nietzsche said was dead. Eliot, in 1923, spoke of the voyage to the Houyhnhnms in *Gulliver's Travels* as "one of the greatest triumphs that the human soul has ever achieved." [20] In *The Waste Land*, Eliot evidently sought to make a similar revelation of the beatitude implied by disgust. [21]

It is not the purpose of this appendix to explicate *The Waste Land*; but perhaps for the sake of completeness, having contemplated the beginning in detail, we might contemplate the end very quickly, noting how the end completes Eliot's design. If we think of the poem as involving a basic desert-garden contrast, and reflect that in Section I, two gardens appear where the protagonist suffers distinctive deaths, we should expect that in Section V a third garden would appear where must occur the death after which there is no other. Everything points to the Chapel Perilous as the Third which interprets the Hofgarten and the Hyacinth garden. The events here are mysterious both in the romances and in *The Waste Land*. According to Jesse Weston, the Quester fails at the Chapel Perilous to achieve something that would have benefited the Fisher King. Jesse Weston, however, also says that the Chapel is a symbol of the first part of an initiation into a mystery, the place of passage through fear of physical death.[22] Eliot's handling of the episode preserves the ambiguities. Something is lost and something is gained. The crowing of the cock seems to tell us that the protagonist has denied his Master for a third time, and, at the same time, to signal that the devils are dispelled; the demons who derive their "plenitude of power" from the protagonist's fears will (by virtue of the shadow of the Rock) have no further dominion over him. By his third denial his eyes are opened. What are they open to? To whatever it is that Harry's eyes are open when (in *The Family Reunion*) instead of fleeing from the Erinyes he turns and pursues them, or Celia's eyes are open (in *The Cocktail Party*) when she chooses the Sanitarium. The protagonist, we might say, sees a new meaning in *The Waste Land*; it becomes the desert between Egypt and the Promised Land. That Land becomes an emblem of the reality of things hoped for and so the protagonist takes his judgment with relief and turns into the new Fisher King whose sufferings are now purgatorial.

To decide how good Eliot's *The Waste Land* is, we might compare it with another triumph of the human spirit, *Gawain and the Green Knight*. Juxtaposing them, we see two great artists with a passion for precise form treating the same quest-theme. One is a product of the medieval community, the other of twentieth-century multiplicity. The Pearl poet sees the beauty of all earthly life, Eliot the horror. "But the essential advantage for a poet is not, to have a beautiful world with which to deal: it is to be able to see beneath both beauty and ugliness; to see the boredom, and the horror, and the glory." [23] Eliot could do this because Josiah Royce and F. H. Bradley taught him how to do so.

NOTES

AFTER THE FIRST REFERENCE, the following abbreviations are used for specific works of T. S. Eliot: C. P. P. (*The Complete Poetry and Plays*); E. O. K. (*Experience and the Objects of Knowledge in the Philosophy of F. H. Bradley*); S. E. (*Selected Essays*); S. W. (*The Sacred Wood*).

Introduction

1. Unpublished letter from James H. Woods, June 23, 1916, prefixed to Eliot's doctoral dissertation in the Houghton Library, Harvard University.

2. Conrad Aiken, *Ushant* (New York, Boston, 1952), p. 215.

3. R. W. Church, "Eliot on Bradley's Metaphysic," *Harvard Advocate*, CXXV (December 1938), 24–26.

4. See Hugh Kenner, *The Invisible Poet: T. S. Eliot* (New York, 1959), p. xiv, where the author acknowledges that he had relied on Henry Ware Eliot's digests and annotations of the manuscript material in the Houghton Library at Harvard that he had been unable to inspect. Kristian Smidt's *Poetry and Belief in the Work of T. S. Eliot* (Oslo, 1949) contains an account of the dissertation that seems to be based on R. W. Church's article.

5. F. H. Bradley, *Appearance and Reality* (Oxford, 1930), p. x.

6. Smidt, *Poetry and Belief in the Work of T. S. Eliot*, p. 33.

7. The idea starts with Eliot himself. See "The Meta-

physical Poets," *Selected Essays* (New York, 1950), p. 248. But interpreters have not noticed, perhaps, that Eliot has just been talking about poets interested in philosophy. (Hereafter, Eliot's *Selected Essays* is referred to as *S. E.*)

8. Soren Kierkegaard, *Fear and Trembling and the Sickness Unto Death*, trans. Walter Lowrie (New York, 1954), p. 59.

9. See, for example, A. Alvarez, *The Shaping Spirit, Studies in Modern English and American Poets* (London, 1958), p. 11. "Eliot and Yeats are our founding fathers; on them our inheritance depends. . . . There is no longer any need for patient elucidation of the texts."

1—Background to the Standpoint

1. See T. S. Eliot, "The Preacher as Artist," *Athenaeum*, 4674 (November 28, 1919), p. 1253, where Eliot speaks of finding in Donne "the artist as an Eye curiously, patiently watching himself as a man." Eliot uses the same image to describe Peter Quilpe's growing to artistic maturity in *The Cocktail Party*. See *The Complete Poems and Plays* (New York, 1952), p. 383. This work is hereafter referred to as *C. P. P.*

2. T. S. Eliot, "Kipling Redivivus," *Athenaeum*, 4645 (May 9, 1919), p. 298. "Mr. Conrad has no ideas, but he has a point of view, a 'world'; it can hardly be defined, but it pervades his work and is unmistakable."

3. T. S. Eliot, "Eeldrop and Appleplex, I," *Little Review*, IV (May 1917), 10. "Our philosophy is quite irrelevant. The essential is, that our philosophy should spring from our point of view and not return upon itself to explain our point of view."

4. George Herbert Mead, *Mind, Self, and Society* (Chicago, 1937), pp. 173–78.

5. See Eliot, "Eeldrop and Appleplex, II," *Little Review*, IV (September 1917), 19. "The artist is part of him a drifter, at the mercy of impressions, and another part

of him allows this to happen for the sake of making use of the unhappy creature." There is also the well-known passage in "Tradition and Individual Talent," *S. E.*, p. 8.

6. Conrad Aiken, "King Bolo and Others," *T. S. Eliot, a Symposium*, compiled by Richard March and Tambimuttu (London, 1948), pp. 20–21.

7. H. T. Costello, "Recollections of Royce's Seminar on Comparative Methodology," *Journal of Philosophy*, LIII (February 2, 1956), 76.

8. Alan Wood, *Bertrand Russell, The Passionate Skeptic* (New York, 1958), p. 94.

9. Wyndham Lewis, "Early London Environment," *T. S. Eliot, a Symposium*, pp. 25–26.

10. Aiken, "King Bolo and Others," p. 22.

11. Wood, *Bertrand Russell*, p. 94.

12. Letter to Wyndham Lewis, July, 1916, *The Letters of Ezra Pound, 1907–1941*, D. D. Paige, ed. (New York, 1950), p. 86.

13. Eliot, "Shakespeare and the Stoicism of Seneca," *S. E.*, p. 108.

14. See Eliot, "The Hawthorne Aspect," *Little Review*, V (August 1918), 51. "The point is that Hawthorne was acutely sensitive to the situation; that he did grasp character through the relation of two or more persons to each other; and this is what no one else, except James, has done." See also "In Memory of Henry James," *Egoist*, V (January 1918), 2. "The focus is a situation, a relation, an atmosphere, to which the characters pay tribute, but being allowed to give only what the writer wants. The real hero, in any of James's stories, is a social entity of which men and women are constituents."

15. Gabriel Marcel, *Man Against Mass Society*, trans. G. S. Fraser (Chicago, 1952), p. 27: ". . . the crisis which Western man is undergoing today is a metaphysical one."

16. See. T. S. Eliot, "Contemporanea," *Egoist*, V (June–July 1918), 84. "When a work of art no longer terrifies us we may know that we were mistaken, or that our senses are dulled: we ought still to find *Othello* or

Lear frightful." See also "Beyle and Balzac," *Athenaeum*,
4648 (May 30, 1919), p. 393. "The surface of existence
coagulates into lumps which look like important simple
feelings, which are identified by names as feelings, which
the patient analyst disintegrates into more complex and
trifling, but ultimately, if he goes far enough, into various
canalizations of something again simple, terrible and unknown."

17. Aiken, "King Bolo and Others," p. 21.

18. Conrad Aiken, *Ushant*, p. 186.

19. Josiah Royce, *The World and the Individual*, First
Series (New York, 1901), p. 138.

20. Jean Desternes, "T. S. Eliot: Interview par Jean
Desternes," *Combat de la Résistance à la Révolution*, 7ᵉ
année numero 1, 182 (vendredi, 23 avril, 1948).

21. Conrad Aiken, "Homage to T. S. Eliot," *Harvard
Advocate*, CXXV (December 1938), 17. "The wholeness
is there from the beginning—and that can be said of perhaps no other living poet. . . . We can—or at any rate
we ought to—regard Eliot's wonderful singleness as something very like a miracle."

22. T. S. Eliot, "A Prediction in Regard to Three English Authors," *Vanity Fair*, XXI (February 1924), 29.
See the same statement in "Lettre d'Angleterre," *La Nouvelle Revue Française*, 11ᵉ année. 122 (1ᵉʳ novembre
1923), 621.

2—*The Metaphysical Standpoint*

1. Eliot, "Francis Herbert Bradley," S. E., p. 404.

2. Henry Adams, *The Education of Henry Adams*
(New York, 1931), p. 451.

3. Eliot, "The 'Pensées' of Pascal," S. E., p. 361

4. Eliot, "Modern Education and the Classics," S. E.,
p. 458.

5. Eliot, *The Use of Poetry* (London, 1934), p. 106.

6. *Sweeney Agonistes*, C. P. P., pp. 80–81.

7. Eliot, "The Function of Criticism," S. E., p. 17.

8. Plato, *The Apology*, Jowett translation, 28.

9. Eliot, *Experience and the Objects of Knowledge in the Philosophy of F. H. Bradley*, p. 211. Hereafter this is referred to as *E. O. K.*

10. See Ralph Barton Perry's criticism of "the egocentric predicament" of the idealistic philosopher in *Present Philosophical Tendencies* (London, Bombay, and Calcutta, 1912), pp. 129 ff.

11. H. T. Costello, "Recollections of Royce's Seminar on Comparative Methodology," *Journal of Philosophy*, LIII (February 2, 1956), 76.

12. *The Letters of John Keats*, ed. Maurice Buxton Forman (London, 1931), II, 342. "Though a quarrel in the streets is a thing to be hated, the energies displayed in it are fine."

13. "Arnold and Pater," *S. E.*, pp. 387–88.

14. Matthew Arnold, "The Study of Poetry," *Essays in Criticism, Second Series* (New York, 1924), p. 2.

15. Charles Baudelaire, "Au lecteur," *Les fleurs du mal.*

16. Eliot, *E. O. K.*, p. 211.

17. *E. O. K.*, p. 98.

18. The maze figures in Eliot's poetry. See *Burnt Norton*, I, and *The Family Reunion*, *C. P. P.*, p. 290. "We do not like the maze in the garden, because it too closely resembles the maze in the brain."

19. Eliot speaks of "point of view" as though it were an "object," but acknowledges that it cannot be such. See *E. O. K.*, p. 189.

20. See Josiah Royce, *The Religious Aspect of Philosophy* (Boston, 1891), p. 424. "*Either there is no such thing as error, which statement is a flat self-contradiction, or else there is an infinite unity of conscious thought to which is present all possible truth.*" (Royce's italics.)

21. F. H. Bradley, *Appearance and Reality* (Oxford, 1930), p. 483. "Still the difference between absolute and finite truth must none the less be upheld. For the former, in a word, is not *intellectually* corrigible."

22. Eliot, "Lettre d'Angleterre," *La Nouvelle Revue Française*, 11ᵉ année. 122 (1ᵉʳ novembre 1923), p. 624.

"Once you accept his theory of the nature of the judgment, and it is as plausible a theory as any, you are led by his arid and highly sensitive eloquence (no English philosopher has ever written finer English) to something which, according to your temperament, will be resignation or despair—the bewildered despair of wondering why you ever wanted anything, and what it was that you wanted, since this philosophy seems to give you everything that you ask and yet to render it not worth wanting." (The translation is taken from the corresponding passage in Eliot's somewhat reduced English version published as "A Prediction in Regard to Three English Authors," *Vanity Fair*, XXI (February 1924), 29 and 98.

23. Plato, *The Republic*, Book I, 336.

24. I have tended to follow the generalized accounts of Bradley's achievements written at the time of his death by thinkers sympathetic to his point of view. See Brand Blanshard, "Francis Herbert Bradley," *Journal of Philosophy*, XXII (January 1925), 5–15; J. H. Muirhead, "Bradley's Place in Philosophy," *Mind*, XXXIV (N.S.) April 1925), 173–83; A. E. Taylor, "F. H. Bradley," *Mind*, XXXIV (1925), 2–12. See also Rudolph Metz, *A Hundred Years of British Philosophy* (London and New York, 1938), pp. 322–62.

25. Bradley, *Ethical Studies* (Oxford, 1927). See "My Station and Its Duties," pp. 160–213.

26. Bradley, *Principles of Logic* (London, 1928), Vol. I, Ch. I, Sect., 18–19; Ch. II, Sect. 1.

27. Bradley, *Appearance and Reality* (Oxford, 1930). See "Introduction." Quotations are from this edition.

28. Eliot, *E. O. K.*, p. 211.

29. Bradley, "On Our Knowledge of Immediate Experience," *Essays on Truth and Reality* (Oxford, 1914), p. 160. "The recognition of the fact of immediate experience opens the one road, I submit, to the solution of ultimate problems."

30. Bradley, *Appearance and Reality*, p. 223: ". . . to find reality, we must betake ourselves to feeling. It is the real, which there appears, which is the subject of all predicates."

31. Eliot, *E. O. K.*, p. 5.

32. *E. O. K.*, p. 24.

33. *E. O. K.*, p. 26.

34. *E. O. K.*, p. 7.

35. *E. O. K.*, p. 6.

36. *E. O. K.*, p.14.

37. *E. O. K.*, p. 13.

38. Bradley, *Appearance and Reality*, p. 306. See *The Waste Land*, *C. P. P.*, p. 54. Eliot's reference is to the early edition of *Appearance and Reality*.

39. *E. O. K.*, p. 22.

40. *E. O. K.*, p. 27. See *Appearance and Reality*, p. 335. "But the union in all perception of thought with sense, the co-presence everywhere in all appearances of fact with ideality—this is the one foundation of truth."

41. *E. O. K.*, p. 61, footnote.

42. *E. O. K.*, pp. 42 and 62. My formulation, here is what I interpret Eliot to be saying. His discussion of "ideas" seems very important for his later work; but it has to be taken as a whole. No single statement can be taken as literally true.

43. *E. O. K.*, p. 61.

44. *E. O. K.*, p. 46.

45. *E. O. K.*, p. 43.

46. *E. O. K.*, pp. 46–47.

47. *E. O. K.*, pp. 98–99.

48. *E. O. K.*, p. 66.

49. *E. O. K.*, p. 66. "Laid out like bricks" is Eliot's image.

50. *E. O. K.*, p. 98.

51. See *E. O. K.*, pp. 105, 133, and 136. My account of Eliot's long and involved chapter is somewhat too free to be even a free translation.

52. I cannot give an exact reference, so I seem to be putting words into Eliot's mouth. The statement, however, seems true to the spirit of the discussion. See *E. O. K.*, p. 103.

53. *E. O. K.*, p. 71.

54. *E. O. K.*, pp. 107 and 137.

55. *E. O. K.*, p. 203.

56. *E. O. K.*, p. 109.

57. *E. O. K.*, p. 109.

58. *E. O. K.*, p. 104.

59. *E. O. K.*, p. 137.

60. *E. O. K.*, p. 203.

61. *E. O. K.*, p. 176.

62. *E. O. K.*, p. 177. See also p. 216.

63. What I had in mind was merely the familiar idea that when the world for us is a "physical world," and nothing more, the "fall" has occurred. I was thinking of William Blake's account of the genesis of the material world as due to failure of vision, and Eliot's "the enchainment of past and future/ Woven in the weakness of the changing body,/ Protects mankind from heaven and damnation/ Which flesh cannot endure." *Burnt Norton*, II, *C. P. P.*, p. 119.

64. *E. O. K.*, p. 183. The illustration of the photographic negative and prints is Eliot's.

65. *E. O. K.*, p. 179.

66. *E. O. K.*, p. 181 ff.

67. *E. O. K.*, p. 184.

68. *E. O. K.*, pp. 23–24.

69. *E. O. K.*, p. 196.

70. *E. O. K.*, p. 191.

71. *E. O. K.*, pp. 186 (a one-page footnote on Leibniz seems to intervene) and 188. See Eliot's "Leibniz's Monads and Bradley's Finite Centers," *The Monist*, XXVI (October 1916), 573. "The self is a construction in space and time."

72. *E. O. K.*, p. 198.

73. *E. O. K.*, pp. 198–99.

74. *E. O. K.*, pp. 191–92.

75. *E. O. K.*, p. 192.

76. *E. O. K.*, p. 193.

77. *E. O. K.*, p. 188.

78. *E. O. K.*, p. 196.

79. *E. O. K.*, p. 197.

80. *E. O. K.*, p. 198.

81. *E. O. K.*, pp. 212–13. In a footnote, Eliot adds that

his materialism is in substance the materialism of Mr. Bosanquet. As everywhere in the dissertation, no single statement can be taken literally.

82. See *E. O. K.*, p. 212 where Eliot speaks of these three together.

83. *E. O. K.*, p. 211.

84. *E. O. K.*, p. 98.

85. *E. O. K.*, p. 211.

86. *E. O. K.*, pp. 211–13.

87. *E. O. K.*, p. 213.

88. Eliot, *C. P. P.*, pp. 125 and 129.

3—The Criticism: 1917–1923

1. "Charles Whibley," *S. E.*, p. 440.

2. "Preface to the 1928 Edition," *The Sacred Wood* (London, 1950), p. viii. This work hereafter is referred to as *S. W.*

3. T. S. Eliot, "The Music of Poetry," *On Poetry and Poets* (New York, 1957), p. 17.

4. T. S. Eliot, *The Use of Poetry*, p. 68.

5. John Hayward's dating of the poems seems to indicate this. "Prufrock," "Portrait of a Lady," "Preludes," "Rhapsody on a Windy Night," "Conversation Galante," and "La Figlia" were written in Cambridge or Paris, 1909–11. "Morning at the Window," "The Boston Evening Transcript," "Aunt Helen," "Mr. Apollinax" were written at Oxford, 1915.

6. See Eliot, "Tradition and the Individual Talent," *S. E.*, p. 4.

7. Eliot, "The Art of Poetry I," *The Paris Review*, No. 21 (Spring-Summer 1959), p. 56.

8. See in *T. S. Eliot: A Selected Critique*, ed. by Leonard Unger (New York, Toronto, 1948), the essay by Yvor Winters, p. 75, and that by John Crowe Ransom, pp. 51–52, 57.

9. *E. O. K.*, pp. 211–13.

10. "The 'Pensées' of Pascal," *S. E.*, p. 367.

11. *The Use of Poetry*, p. 68.

12. Friedrich Nietzsche, *The Birth of Tragedy*, trans. Francis Golffing (New York, 1956), pp. 136–37.

13. Eliot, "Literature, Science, and Dogma," *Dial*, LXXII (March 1927), 239.

14. *The Use of Poetry*, p. 143.

15. See René Wellek, "The Criticism of T. S. Eliot," *Sewanee Review*, LXIV (Summer 1956), 400. "Eliot has been constantly working at a general theory, and from the very beginning has had a theory in the back of his mind."

16. See *S. E.*, pp. 10, 50, 117, 124, 192, 269, 276, 285.

17. "Religion and Literature," *S. E.*, p. 343. "In so far as in any age there is common agreement on ethical and theological matters, so far can literary criticism be substantive." My application involves, I am afraid, a modification of Eliot's meaning.

18. H. T. Costello, "Recollections of Royce's Seminar on Comparative Methodology," *Journal of Philosophy*, LIII (February 2, 1956), 76.

19. See especially "Conscience and Christ. . . ." and "Group Theories of Religion and the Religion of the Individual" in *International Journal of Ethics*, XXVII (October 1916), 111–12, 115–16; "Mens Creatrix" and "Religion and Philosophy," XXVII (July 1917), 542–43, 543.

20. T. S. Eliot, *Notes Toward a Definition of Culture* (New York, 1949), p. 29. "To judge a work of art by artistic or by religious standards, to judge a religion by religious or artistic standards should come in the end to the same thing: though it is an end at which no individual can arrive."

21. *E. O. K.*, pp. 42–43.

22. Matt. 12:36–37.

23. *E. O. K.*, p. 11.

24. "The Possibility of a Poetic Drama," *S. W.*, pp. 64–65.

25. "William Blake," *S. E.*, p. 275.

26. Cf. Leonard Unger, *The Man in the Name* (Minneapolis, 1956), p. 133. See also Eliot, *S. W.*, pp. 11 and 70.

27. See "Rudyard Kipling," *On Poetry and Poets*, p. 279, footnote.

28. R. G. Collingwood, *The Principles of Art* (New York, 1958), pp. 228–34.

29. Collingwood, pp. 212–13.

30. Collingwood, p. 246.

31. Collingwood, p. 226.

32. Eliot, "Studies in Contemporary Criticism I," *Egoist*, V (October 1918), 114.

33. Samuel H. Butcher, *Aristotle's Theory of Poetry and Fine Art* (London, 1923), pp. 7 and 23.

34. Longinus, *On the Sublime*, IX.

35. Josiah Royce, *The Spirit of Modern Philosophy* (Boston and New York, 1892), pp. 391–96.

36. I. A. Richards, *Science and Poetry* (New York, 1926), Chapter V.

37. *C. P. P.*, p. 136.

38. "The Perfect Critic," *S. W.*, pp. 14–15.

39. *S. E.*, pp. 8 and 247.

40. See *Coleridge's Literary Criticism*, introd. by J. W. Mackail (London, 1908), pp. 176–77 or the passage in *Biographia Literaria*, Ch. XIV.

41. *C. P. P.*, p. 307.

42. See *S. E.*, pp. 117, 259. "Beyle and Balzac," *Athenaeum*, 4648 (May 30, 1919), p. 392, makes the point strongly: "Dostoevsky's point of departure is always a human brain in a human environment, and the 'aura' is simply the continuation of the quotidian experience of the brain into seldom explored extremities of torture." Eliot is critical of Balzac's failure to start with the really actual.

43. "Beyle and Balzac," *Athenaeum*, 4648 (May 30, 1919), pp. 392–93.

44. Eliot, I am afraid, does not actually say what I infer. But see "Dante," *S. E.*, pp. 208 and 212.

45. "Andrew Marvell," *S. E.*, p. 262.

46. Matthew Arnold, "The Function of Criticism at the Present Time," *Essays in Criticism, First Series* (New York, 1924), p. 7. Eliot commends Arnold's insight in *The Use of Poetry*, p. 104.

47. *C. P. P.*, p. 305.

48. *S. W.*, p. 15, and "Reflections on Contemporary Poetry, III," *Egoist*, IV (November 1917), 151. "The writers in *The New Poetry* who have avoided rhetoric . . . have done so chiefly by the exercise, in greater or less degree, of intelligence, of which an important function is the discernment of exactly what, and how much, we feel in any given situation."

49. T. S. Eliot, *After Strange Gods* (New York, 1934), p. 63. Also *S. E.*, p. 262.

50. *S. E.*, p. 279, and *After Strange Gods*, p. 63.

51. *S. W.*, pp. 62–64. For some other examples of Eliot's use of the word "form," see *S. E.*, pp. 375 and 93.

52. "The Poetic Drama," *Athenaeum*, 4698 (May 14, 1920), p. 635.

53. Josiah Royce, *The Problem of Christianity* (New York, 1913), I, 164 ff.

54. *S. E.*, p. 9.

55. In "Reflections on Contemporary Poetry," *Egoist*, VI (July 1919), 39, Eliot describes how a "feeling of profound kinship, or rather of a peculiar personal intimacy, with another, probably a dead author" may change a writer "within a few weeks even, from a bundle of second-hand sentiments into a person."

56. Nietzsche, *The Birth of Tragedy*, VIII.

57. *S. W.*, p. 63.   58. *S. E.*, p. 247.

59. *S. E.*, p. 273.

60. *Appearance and Reality*, p. 335.

61. *S. E.*, p. 273.

62. *S. E.*, pp. 285 and 273.

63. *S. E.*, pp. 278–79.

64. *S. E.*, pp. 277 and 294. See also "Verse Pleasant and Unpleasant," *Egoist*, V (March 1918), 43: "And Tennyson had a brain (a large dull brain like a farmhouse clock) which saved him from triviality."

65. *S. E.*, p. 280.

66. Compare Eliot's remarks on Shakespeare and Montaigne, *S. E.*, p. 126, and those on Pascal and Montaigne, *S. E.*, pp. 362–63. See also *S. E.*, p. 294.

67. "Four Elizabethan Dramatists," *S. E.*, p. 93.

68. For Eliot on the relation of "realism," "form," and religion, see "A Dialogue on Dramatic Poetry," *S. E.*, p. 37.

69. "Lettre d'Angleterre," *La Nouvelle Revue Française*, 11ᵉ année 122 (1ᵉʳ novembre 1923), 619–25. Hereafter referred to as *N. R. F.*

70. So I interpret Eliot's praise of the purity of Bradley's philosophy in contrast to that of Bergson, which contains an unexamined faith in biology, and that of Russell, which contains an unexamined commitment to mathematics. See *N. R. F.*, 623.

71. *S. E.*, pp. 128 and 135. *S. W.*, p. 117.

72. "Beyle and Balzac," *Athenaeum*, 4648 (May 30, 1919), p. 392.

73. "The Metaphysical Poets," *S. E.*, p. 247.

74. "Reflections on Contemporary Poetry, II," *Egoist*, IV (October 1917), 133. "Instead of refining ordinary human emotion (and I do not mean tepid human emotion, but human, however intense—in the crude living state) he [the intellectual poet] aims direct at emotions of art. . . . The effect is sometimes an intense frigidity, which I find altogether admirable."

75. "The Noh and the Image," *Egoist*, IV (August 1917), 103.

76. *S. E.*, p. 138.

77. "The Method of Mr. Pound," *Athenaeum*, 4669 (October 24, 1919), p. 1065.

78. "Ulysses, Order and Myth," *Dial*, LXXV (November 1923), 480–83.

79. *N. R. F.*, p. 621. See the English version from *Vanity Fair* (February 1924,) p. 29, quoted at the end of Chapter 1.

80. *N. R. F.*, 622.

81. See Eliot, "London Letter," *Dial*, LXXI (October 1921), 453. "Even *The Golden Bough* can be read in two ways: as a collection of entertaining myths, or as a revelation of that vanished mind of which our mind is a continuation."

4—Burnt Norton

1. Grover Smith, Jr., *T. S. Eliot's Poetry and Plays* (Chicago, 1956), p. 251.

2. George Williamson, *A Reader's Guide to T. S. Eliot* (New York, 1953), p. 208.

3. F. O. Matthiessen, *The Achievement of T. S. Eliot* (New York and London, 1947), p. 183.

4. Smith, *T. S. Eliot's Poetry and Plays*, p. 299.

5. *The Use of Poetry*, p. 152. "I myself should like an audience which could neither read nor write."

6. See "Rhetoric and Poetic Drama," *S. E.*, pp. 27–28. "The really fine rhetoric of Shakespeare occurs in situations where a character in a play *sees himself* in a dramatic light. . . . And in the rhetorical speeches from Shakespeare which have been cited, we have this necessary advantage of a new clue to the character, in noting the angle from which he views himself."

7. Eliot, "The Three Voices of Poetry," *On Poetry and Poets*, p. 98. "It may be, as I have read, that there is a dramatic element in much of my early work. It may be that from the beginning I aspired unconsciously to the theatre."

8. Eliot, "Dante," *S. E.*, p. 207.

9. *The Family Reunion*, *C. P. P.*, p. 247.

10. Karl Shapiro, "T. S. Eliot: The Death of Literary Judgment," *Saturday Review*, XLIV (February 27, 1960), 35.

11. Celia in *The Cocktail Party*, *C. P. P.*, p. 326.

12. Harry does not use these words. But see *C. P. P.*, p. 249, "the legion of the hopeless."

13. Jean-Paul Sartre, *Literary Essays*, trans. Annette Michelson (New York, 1957), p. 82.

14. *C. P. P.*, p. 258.

15. *C. P. P.*, p. 256.

16. *C. P. P.*, p. 365.

17. *Pascal's Pensées*, introd. by T. S. Eliot (New York, 1948), p. 121.

18. *C. P. P.*, p. 234.

19. Eliot, *Use of Poetry*, p. 69. "The author of *Biographia Literaria* was already a ruined man. Sometimes, however, to be a 'ruined man' is itself a vocation."

20. Agatha in *The Family Reunion*, C. P. P., p. 229.

21. See *The Birth of Tragedy*, VII, the last two paragraphs.

22. C. P. P., p. 356.

23. Eliot, "Henry James," *Egoist*, V (January 1918), 1–2; reprinted in Edmund Wilson, *The Shock of Recognition* (Garden City, N. Y., 1947), p. 857.

24. Eliot, "Preface," *Anabasis* (New York, 1949), p. 10. "The reader should take at least as much trouble as a barrister reading an important decision on a complicated case."

25. C. P. P., p. 327.

26. C. P. P., p. 362.

27. See Smith, *T. S. Eliot's Poetry and Plays*, p. 256. Smith himself is doubtful "whether these children are the same as 'they.'"

28. C. P. P., p. 266.

29. C. P. P., p. 277.

30. C. P. P., p. 257. If "ghosts" are unfulfilled intentions, Harry might be said to be pursued by the ghosts of what Amy, Agatha, and Harry's first wife intended. Mary in that case is the embodiment of Amy's intention. If we count Mary there are four ghosts as in *Murder in the Cathedral*.

31. See again Smith, *T. S. Eliot's Poetry and Plays*, p. 256. The relation of Rudyard Kipling's "They" to this section, I do not fully follow. The story is relevant, as Helen Gardner, *The Art of T. S. Eliot* (New York, 1950), p. 160, has pointed out.

32. "Milton II," *On Poetry and Poets*, p. 177.

33. Paul Tillich, *Systematic Theology* (Chicago, 1957), II, 29–30.

34. C. P. P., p. 229.

35. See Matthiessen's *The Achievement of T. S. Eliot*, p. 24, for Eliot's remarks on James's effort to present evil in "The Turn of the Screw."

36. Ananda K. Coomaraswamy, "Primordial Images," *PMLA*, LXI (June 1946), 601–2.

37. C. P. P., p. 277.

38. C. P. P., p. 277.

39. "Lotus," *Dictionary of Folklore, Mythology, and Legend* (New York, 1950).

40. Philip Wheelwright, *The Burning Fountain, A Study in the Language of Symbolism* (Bloomington, Indiana, 1954), pp. 127 and 320.

41. C. P. P., p. 208.

42. Cf. Leonard Unger, "T. S. Eliot's Rose Garden," *T. S. Eliot: A Selected Critique*, p. 384: "Privacy is spoiled by an 'unseen eyebeam' and the roses have the 'look of flowers that are looked at.' "

43. S. E., p. 29.

44. Eliot, *After Strange Gods*, pp. 65–66: "His [Lawrence's] early belief in Life may have passed over, as a really serious belief in Life must, into a belief in Death."

45. C. P. P., p. 324.

46. See, for example, Dante, *Paradiso*, XVIII, 25.

47. C. P. P., p. 182.

48. C. P. P., p. 268.

49. John Betjeman, "The Usher of Highgate Junior School," *T. S. Eliot, A Symposium* (London, 1948), p. 90.

50. "Milton I," *On Poetry and Poets*, p. 163.

51. Mark Reinsberg, "A Footnote to *Four Quartets*," *American Literature*, XXI (November 1949), 343–44.

52. "In Memory of Major Robert Gregory," *The Collected Poems of W. B. Yeats* (New York, 1951), p. 130.

53. Soren Kierkegaard, *Fear and Trembling and the Sickness unto Death*, trans. Walter Lowrie (New York, 1954), p. 59.

54. C. P. P., p. 382.

55. Josiah Royce, *The World and the Individual*, Second Series (New York, 1901), 359 ff. "The sole possible free moral action is then a freedom that relates to the present fixing of attention upon the ideas of the Ought which are already present. To sin is *consciously to choose*

to forget, through a narrowing of the field of attention, an Ought that one already recognizes."

56. *C. P. P.*, p. 275.

57. Saint John of the Cross, *Dark Night of the Soul*, Book II, Ch. XIX–XX, pp. 463–70, *The Complete Works*, I, trans. and ed. by E. Allison Peers (London, 1947).

58. A. E. Taylor, *Plato* (New York, 1927), p. 225.

59. *S. E.*, p. 6.

60. Eliot, *On Poetry and Poets*, p. 94.

61. Royce, *The Problem of Christianity* (New York, 1913), I, 211.

5—Appendix: The Waste Land

1. Northrop Frye, *Anatomy of Criticism, Four Essays* (Princeton, 1957), p. 4.

2. *C. P. P.*, p. 235 and p. 269.

3. *C. P. P.*, p. 268.

4. "Thoughts After Lambeth," *S. E.*, p. 324. "I dislike the word 'generation,' which has been a talisman for the last ten years; when I wrote a poem called *The Waste Land* some of the more approving critics said that I had expressed the 'disillusionment of a generation,' which is nonsense. I may have expressed for them their own illusion of being disillusioned, but that did not form part of my intention."

5. Richard Chase, "T. S. Eliot in Concord," *American Scholar*, XVI (Autumn 1947), 441. Mr. Chase reports Eliot's remarks in a brief Commencement Address at Concord Academy, Concord, Massachusetts, June 3, 1947. "He had written *The Waste Land* 'to relieve my emotions,' a purely personal act."

6. "Shakespeare and the Stoicism of Seneca," *S. E.*, p. 117.

7. E. S. Eliot, "The Noh and the Image," *Egoist*, IV (August 1917), 102. The protagonist's states of mind (Awoi's "ghosts") are projected directly on stage, with-

out, as in *Hamlet*, the representation of a castle on a frosty night; Awoi's illness is symbolized simply by a pink kimona at the front of the stage. In occidental drama, Eliot says, we have more help *from* imagination, in Japanese more help *for* it. This is to say, in Noh plays, there is less help in *reviving* an experience, more help in reviving its *meaning*. "The peculiarity of the Noh is that the focus of interest, the centre of construction is the scene *on-the-stage*." This is the peculiarity of *The Waste Land*.

8. Letter to T. S. Eliot, December 24, 1921, *The Letters of Ezra Pound*, *1907–1941*, p. 169.

9. Friedrich Nietzsche, *The Birth of Tragedy*, VIII, Francis Golffing, trans. (New York, 1956). "The chorus is the 'ideal spectator' inasmuch as it is the only *seer*." (P. 54.) "Since, in this vision, the chorus beholds its lord and master Dionysos, it remains forever an *attending* chorus; it sees how the god suffers and transforms himself, and it has, for that reason, no need to act." (P. 57.) Teresias is to *The Waste Land* what The Rock is in "Choruses from *The Rock*." In introducing The Rock, Eliot uses imagery and language practically identical with that Sophocles uses to introduce Teresias in *Oedipus Tyrannus*.

Eliot:

> *For I perceive approaching*
>
> . . . .
> *The God-shaken, in whom is truth inborn.*
> *Enter the* Rock, *led by a* Boy. (C. P. P., p. 97).

Sophocles (F. Storrs, trans., London, 1916, I, 29):

> *Lo, at length*
> *They bring the god-inspirèd seer in whom*
> *Above all other men is truth inborn.*
> *Enter* Teresias *led by a boy.*

Gerontion, being read to by a boy, is another image of The Rock, the Stranger. Eliot considered (as Pound's letters indicate) prefixing "Gerontion" to *The Waste Land*. What Teresias sees in *The Waste Land* is the *commu-*

nity that is violated by the young man who makes "a welcome of indifference" and the pathetic girl who is "glad it's over." This community is the "infinitely gentle, infinitely suffering thing" of "Preludes."

10. *Birth of Tragedy*, VII. "The truth once seen, man is aware everywhere of the ghastly absurdity of existence, comprehends the symbolism of Ophelia's fate and the wisdom of the wood sprite Silenus: nausea invades him.

"Then, in this supreme jeopardy of the will, art, that sorceress expert in healing, approaches him; only she can turn his fits of nausea into imaginations with which it is possible to live." (pp. 51–52.) Although Eliot's review of A. Wolfe's "The Philosophy of Nietzsche," (*International Journal of Ethics*, XXVI [April 1916], 426–27) shows him distrustful of this thinker, *The Birth of Tragedy* is a powerful presence in *The Waste Land*. Consider Nietzsche's "Suddenly we see only Tristan, lying motionless and torpid, and hear him ask, 'Why does that familiar strain waken me?' And what before had seemed a hollow sigh echoing from the womb of things now says to us simply, 'Waste and empty the sea.' " (Golffing, trans., p. 128). Compare it with Eliot's Wagner passage in Section I. Or compare Nietzsche's "What else, in the desolate waste of present-day culture, holds any promise of a sound healthy future? In vain we look for a single powerfully branching root, a spot of earth that is fruitful: we see only dust, sand, dullness and languor" (p. 123) with Eliot's "What are the roots that clutch . . . ?" In Section V, Eliot's "But who is that on the other side of you?" seems a reminiscence of Nietzsche's, "In such hopeless isolation no better symbol comes to mind than that of 'The Knight, Death, and the Devil' of Dürer, the steely-eyed armored knight who pursues his dreadful path, undismayed by his ghastly companions and yet without hope, alone with horse and dog" (p. 123). There are other such echoes. Nietzsche possibly was a symbol of something romantic in himself that the poet in *The Waste Land* was purging.

11. *The Family Reunion, C. P. P.*, p. 275.

12. See Ralph Withington Church, *Bradley's Dialectic*

(London, 1942), p. 6. There is a "middle between any two co-opposites."

13. See especially Josiah Royce, *The Problem of Christianity*, II, p. 188. "As the tragic artist looks down upon the many varying lives of his characters, and sees their various motives not interpenetrating, but cooperating, in the dramatic action which constitutes his creation,—so anyone who compares distinct ideas, and discovers the third or mediating idea which interprets the meaning of one in the light of the other, thereby discovers, or invents, a realm of conscious unity which constitutes the very essence of the life of reason."

14. Eliot, *The Use of Poetry*, p. 124.

15. See *Murder in the Cathedral*, C. P. P., p. 181.

16. "Dante," S. W., p. 168.

17. Jean Guitton, *Essay on Human Love*, Melville Chaning-Pearce, trans. (New York, 1951), pp. 34–35.

18. Eliot, "A Commentary," *Criterion*, XII (April 1934), 452.

19. *The Cocktail Party*, C. P. P., p. 364.

20. "Ulysses, Order, and Myth," *Dial*, LXXV (November 1923), 480.

21. See "Dante," S. W., p. 169. "The contemplation of the horrid or sordid or disgusting, by an artist, is the necessary and negative aspect of the impulse toward the pursuit of beauty." See also "The 'Pensées' of Pascal," S. E., p. 364. "But it [Pascal's despair] was also a despair which was a necessary prelude to, and element in, the joy of faith." See finally, "Baudelaire," S. E., p. 379. "The poetry of flight . . . is . . . a dim recognition of the direction of beatitude."

22. Jesse L. Weston, *From Ritual to Romance* (New York, 1957), p. 176 and p. 182.

23. Eliot, *The Use of Poetry*, p. 106.